STANDING TALL

By Paul Harasim

WRS
PUBLISHING
A Division of WRS Group, Inc.
Waco, Texas

First published in the United States of America in 1993 by WRS Publishing,
A Division of WRS Group, Inc., 701 N. New Road, Waco, Texas 76710
Book design by Kenneth Turbeville
Jacket design by Talmage Minter
Front jacket photo source—Michael Boddy of the *Houston Post*
Back jacket from the Church family collection

10 9 8 7 6 5 4 3 2 1

Library of Congress Cataloging-in-Publication Data

Harasim, Paul, 1947-
    Standing tall / by Paul Harasim.
        p.   cm.
    ISBN 1-56796-017-0 : $12.95
    1. Church, Tucker, 1974-   . 2. Little League baseball—Texas—
Houston. 3. Sports for physically handicapped children. 4. Cerebral
palsied children—United States—Biography. I. Title.
GV880.5.H37 1993
796.357'62'092—dc20
    [B]   93-26592
                                                            CIP

Acknowledgement

*To my parents, William and Jean Harasim,
my wife, Teresa, and my children, Isaiah, Sonja, and
Tatiana: Thank you for helping me stand tall.*

Foreword

I first read about Tucker when my good friend, Paul Harasim of the *Houston Post*, wrote a column about him in 1989. We're both from Houston. Right off I had a special feeling for Tucker. He was kicked off his Little League team because he was too old, and for the last six years they've been trying to kick me out of boxing because they think I'm too old, too.

But neither Tucker nor I believed 'em. I'll admit I haven't quite gotten my heavyweight title back yet, but Tucker is now champion of the world in my eyes and in the hearts of millions of Americans. They tell me that Tucker got over fifty thousand letters when *Reader's Digest* wrote up his story in its "Today's Hero's" section. I hate to admit it, but that's more letters than I got the whole time I was heavyweight champ, and I'm supposed to be the world's biggest marketer—no pun intended.

Maybe there's another reason I like Tucker Church—because his name is Church. While I love boxing like Tucker loves baseball, church work is my really big thing.

I believe goodness truly is its own blessing, and Tucker Church is a good young man. He has shown courage, concern, and caring, and it's all paying off in his own life and in the changes in all our attitudes about the abilities of the disabled. Little League is better off today because of Tucker Church. Jackie Robinson would be as proud of him as I am.

One last thing, I know Tucker Church is supposed to be the hero of this book, but don't forget his mother and dad and the Houston Shriners Hospital. I'll never forget the Shriners because they helped my little brother Kenneth when he got polio. And folks like me and Tucker should never forget our mothers. God bless 'em!

—George Foreman

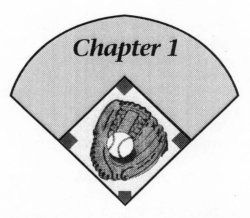

Chapter 1

Cerebral palsy would take from Tucker Church any chance of hitting a baseball like Babe Ruth or throwing one like Nolan Ryan. For that matter, the condition that tied his muscles in knots wouldn't even give him a chance to hit and throw like Joe Lyons, his good buddy down the street.

At fifteen, Tucker didn't quite stand four foot nine inches tall—the cerebral palsy had left him in a semi-squat. Even with a sweaty baseball uniform on and a bat in his hand, he weighed less than fifty-six pounds. But that didn't stop the skinny boy with the twisted, matchstick legs and arms from dreaming. Back then, baseball was his only field of dreams. Maybe in his next Little League game his life would change; his body would loosen up and do what he wanted. At night as he lay sleeping, and often as he stood out in center field, he didn't see himself striking out over and over again. He didn't see himself tripping over his feet on the way to first base. He didn't see himself misjudging a pop fly and breaking his nose.

What the little left-hander saw in his dreams was someone he had never been, a leader, a guy everyone wanted to be like. His knees and feet weren't turned in, his butt didn't stick way out, and nobody at school called him a cripple or said he ran like a chicken. He was standing tall.

Nobody ever called him a cripple on the baseball field.

Not once. Nobody ever laughed at him there either. It wasn't like school at all. It got so that even opposing players cheered when he threw out one of their players at first. Kids can be mean, but they can be understanding, too.

The baseball field had become the one place where Tucker always felt comfortable. When his grades started slipping in sixth grade because he couldn't take notes fast enough—his writing hand simply didn't have the required dexterity—baseball took on a far greater meaning than it had before. Until his problems with note-taking, he had also felt like one of the gang in the classroom. His mind was agile and his A and B grades had reflected that. He liked the idea of what former President Kennedy said—"Ask not what your country can do for you; ask what you can do for your country"—so much that he wrote a paper on it and thought about going into politics. He could see himself using his office to really help people help themselves. But as he fell further and further behind on his note-taking, only on the baseball field did he feel truly content.

The dreams he had experienced as an eight-year-old became more intense at twelve, thirteen, fourteen, and fifteen years of age. He saw himself running so fast that he could beat out a routine ground ball to shortstop. And then he'd steal second and third and come home on a squeeze bunt. He'd break up double plays like the Houston Astros' fiery second baseman, Billy Doran—plowing into the shortstop so hard at second that he'd drop the ball. Home runs would leave his bat in clutch situations. He could see himself up with his team down by a run in the ninth, and he'd tag a two-run shot over the left-field fence. His teammates would mob him and his hand would get sore from too many high-fives. He would throw out a runner at second from the outfield fence. If he played second, he would backhand a scorching line drive, step on second to double up a runner halfway between second and third and then throw to first to complete a triple play.

In those dreams everything else fell into place, too. Nobody mocked his gait or called him "crip" as he walked down the hallway in school. Note taking was a breeze, so classes were, too. There was no need to be shy about girls, to wonder if they'd go out with a guy with hitches in his walk. Cheerleaders liked him, so did the girls in the school play. He could go hunting with his father, even join the Army if he wanted.

As he readied himself in 1989 for what he figured would be his last year of organized baseball—he understood that barring a miracle he wouldn't have the coordination to play at a higher level—the boy would awaken in the morning and stretch to see if his body had changed. But the tightness was always there. He'd try to push his legs straight out and the effort would leave him breathing hard. Sometimes he wondered if his legs would snap like a rubber band if he kept it up. As frustrating as the ritual was, he didn't let it get him down. He knew there probably wouldn't be any miraculous transformation because his older sister still had her cerebral palsy. But somehow, playing Little League had made him think anything was possible. Hadn't he once circled all the bases after hitting the ball?

Tucker had learned what it was like to win and to lose as part of a team. He was grateful for that. Like most teenagers, he wasn't sure of many things in life. But he was sure of one thing: Little League would never let him down.

That's what made it so much harder to take when Little League did.

On May 24, 1989, Tucker's parents were told he couldn't play any more. The long-standing, up-front agreement they had had with a local Little League to let Tucker play with boys his own size rather than his own age—supported unanimously by the League's board for safety reasons—was ruled impermissible by higher Little League officials. The news hurt Tucker. Badly. His parents were outraged. So, it turned out, was the nation. Especially when it was learned that Little League officials—always quick to spout the line that "rules are rules are rules"—had withheld information about the organization's age-waiver process.

The Church family's clash with Little League struck a nerve across the country. These weren't people engaging in the great American pastime of looking around for someone else to blame for their problems. They were getting the shaft from an uncaring bureaucracy. Newspapers, TV, and radio told the story. Commentators editorialized, talk show hosts fanned the emotional flames. The Churches couldn't believe the reaction. There were calls from reporters around the world. The Japanese were interested. So were the Mexicans and the English. Telegrams and letters and phone calls of support poured in. Canadians got on the phone to see if there was anything they could do.

Judi Church was stunned. "Other disabled kids are having a tough time just staying alive," she said.

True, but they weren't having to fight an organization ostensibly set up for the enjoyment of children.

The outpouring of concern and anger generated by Little League's treatment of Tucker was one of those glorious moments in American life when you saw clearly that despite much comfort, plenty, and security—what writer John Steinbeck referred to as "the destroyers of nations"—Americans had yet to become so cynical and so bored that they would tolerate the lack of fair play.

There were some, of course, who wondered, and may still wonder, if a brouhaha involving Little League warranted such heavy public debate, if it wasn't much ado about nothing. Those people obviously don't understand the role of Little League in the raising of American children.

Little League is supposed to be as American as apple pie, supposed to illustrate to children the positive aspects of competition—the very backbone of America. Two and a half million children now play it every year. Many millions more have played and enjoyed the game. Often, they have made friends there that lasted a lifetime. It has been a beautiful rite of passage for so many. Executives can remember their first home runs, their first running catches; so can warehousemen and plumbers. To see Little League go so sour was akin to seeing a church official stealing from the poor. Was nothing sacred?

"Whoever wants to know the heart and mind of America had better learn baseball," wrote the French-born educator Jacques Barzun. Yes, baseball has mirrored America's sometimes agonizing growth. Civil rights gains, the westward migration, the South rising again, greed at its worst—it's never hard to find a reflection of American life in big league baseball.

But who would have ever thought that baseball on the Little League level, where children are supposedly divorced from the harshest realities of life, would reflect the worst in America today—selfishness, bigotry, and the mad scramble for power?

When the Tucker Church affair came to light, it became obvious that not just a few parents were the problem. Institutionalized callousness seemed obvious. Why in the world would officials bother a handicapped child who was trying to have fun, particularly when there was an age-rule waiver available for just that kind of situation? It certainly appeared that the people in charge just didn't want to be hassled with accommodating a disabled child. Instead of being a force for good, the Little League brass seemed bent on showing that the institution not only had warts, but actually encouraged their growth. That's why people got so angry, so concerned. This wasn't the Little League they knew, where fun and caring for a child's welfare were paramount. Not just one winning-isn't-everything-it's-the-only-thing parent had told Tucker Church to get lost. So had the top national officials.

If enough public pressure hadn't been brought to bear to make Little League rethink its position, a child who ran and threw a little differently would have been treated like a leper. That wasn't the kind of Little League people envisioned for their children. That wasn't a lesson most parents wanted their children to learn.

Because of what happened to Tucker, many lives other than Tucker's, were changed. As so often happens in daily journalism, the public only received what amounted to tiny snapshots of the boy and his family. As compelling as the snapshots were, as sad and angry and, finally, as good as they made people feel, they were only leads to a much larger and much more important story, one that lifts the human spirit even as it shows how the men now running Little League baseball in Williamsport, Pennsylvania, too often try to destroy it.

Few know, for example, the huge impact Tucker's battle with Little League had on disabled persons. And because the national brass settled out of court for more than one million dollars with the family of a coach who was beaten to death on the playing field, it never came to light that Little League's treatment of Tucker was a key element in a case that pointed to institutionalized callousness— intolerable behavior by the Little League hierarchy that has yet to stop; outrageous conduct that should make millions of American parents wonder whether it is wise to allow Little League to remain on its present course.

Tucker's parents, Terry and Judi Church, who fought their battle with Little League only in the court of public opinion, would certainly argue that it's unwise.

That they not only had the energy to fight an unfeeling bureaucracy but used the struggle to strengthen their son as well is testimony to their resilience. Unfortunately, even some of the most doting parents have their strength sapped as they work to overcome the bigotry their disabled children face. And then they suffer in silence, shutting themselves and their children off from mainstream America. The Churches' lives, so filled with pain that you wonder how they still manage to spread joy to others, give us fine examples to emulate.

With two of their six children having disabilities, the Churches could have long ago squandered their lives, and those of their children, in self-pity and bitterness. Virtually everyone would have understood. No one would have blamed them. How much, after all, can people take? But they kept their faith in the future.

They know all too well that awful things can occur and too often do without any seeming justice. And they know that some people, because of ignorance or selfishness or cruelty, can be merciless toward those who are different. But they continue to believe that there are others, many others, who are good and decent and more than willing to welcome you with open arms, willing to try and help you over a hurdle that may seem too high.

Didn't the Shriners, after reading about a disabled youngster's battle with Little League, seek out Tucker so he could get free corrective surgery? Didn't the Houston Astros react to the ugliness of Little League by inviting Tucker to throw out the first pitch against the Los Angeles Dodgers? Didn't New Yorkers—to protest Little League's attitude toward handicapped children—raise the money to fly the Church family to their city for a Tucker Church Day? Didn't the heads of the insurance industry's prestigious Million Dollar Roundtable ask Tucker and Judi to address their membership because they felt that the story of their lives was inspirational?

The glass is half-full, not half-empty, the Churches tell their children. Embrace life, enjoy it, make the most of it. That Tucker Church has managed to take these lessons to heart and has begun working toward a broadcasting career should give us all hope. That his journey to find his own path in life has been made all the more difficult because of insensitivity and discrimination should give us all pause.

When Tucker says, "I just wish people would remember not to cripple the disabled," we must listen. Yes, it's true that Congress, in an effort to combat discrimination against the disabled, passed the Americans with Disabilities Act. But a change in attitudes can't be legislated. That will come only because we finally understand the far-reaching effects of discrimination. America is at risk only because it does not give all its people the opportunity to realize their full potential.

Shortly after forty-seven-year-old Jimmy Lee Norwood drove through a torrential downpour to drop his wife off at work, his waterlogged car stalled. As he pushed it into the parking lot of a Houston donut shop, Norwood gasped as the all-too-familiar pain began to tear through his chest.

It was the retired personnel director's fifth heart attack in ten years. Passers-by watched as medics at the scene worked frantically on the man with the diseased heart. When he passed out, he couldn't be revived.

At Norwood's funeral in July 1989, there were some who wondered why the Norwood family asked that donations go to the Texas Special Olympics instead of the American Heart Association.

"Not everyone knew how moved my son had been about Tucker Church," said a tearful, sixty-nine-year-old Glyn Norwood. "Jimmy decided he wanted to do all he could to make sure that Tucker and all other kids with handicaps had a chance to participate in sports. This is our way of honoring our boy and Tucker Church."

The scene at the funeral home left little doubt as to the impact of Little League's behavior toward a handicapped boy. Mourners told Norwood's relatives how wonderful it was that he had tried to right a wrong against a child he had never even met. "Your son knew what was important in life," one woman said.

Norwood, whose heart operated only at thirty-nine percent of capacity, called me on May 26, 1989, the day I published the first story about Tucker. Upset about what had happened to Tucker, this man who never had any children was also stunned that Little League officials were banning Tucker's coach, Scott Davis, from ever coaching again. (Davis had felt it was safer for the fifteen-year-old youngster with cerebral palsy to compete with boys twelve and under.)

"This is the first time in my life that I can say I'm ashamed to be a Texan," Norwood drawled.

A former Little League coach, Norwood phoned local, state, and national Little League officials and gave them an earful. He dialed friends and told them to get on Little League's case, too. He called talk shows and said people had to pressure Little League into working for youngsters, not against them.

Norwood didn't have a well heart, but he did have a big one.

The last time I talked with him he asked me a question I couldn't answer.

"Why do people handicap the handicapped?"

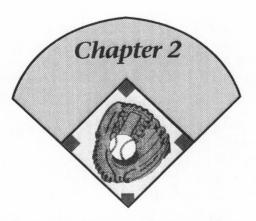

Chapter 2

They become forever etched in our memories—a first love, a first job, the death of a parent, the birth of a child... the benchmarks of our lives, the times that help define why we have become who we are. Graduations, varsity letters, marriages, promotions—while we obviously don't all have precisely the same points of reference or the same feelings to accompany them, there are enough similarities among most Americans to give us the sense that we're all in this together. Yet when Tucker Church sifts through his memory to find the moments that most shaped him, you are struck not by the commonality of his experience, but by its dissimilarity. And you wonder how he, and other disabled youngsters, find the strength to keep on keepin' on.

Even after the corrective procedures that have largely lifted him out of his energy-draining, semi-squatting gait, you become aware of a hip-hop to his still pigeon-toed walk. His head goes up and down with each stride, as though there's a pogo stick attached to his spine. The hop's not as severe as before, but it's still there. When he throws a ball, his elbow almost seems connected to his side, so his delivery becomes more of a forearm fling. You notice these things only because you look hard. Otherwise, his smile, that wonderful smile that says it's great to be alive, magically erases everything else from your vision. In a society where so many are so uptight about appearance that even the slightly obese and barely pimply-faced are targets for taunts, he's had to take people's cruelest insults. And he's come away smiling. But don't think it's been easy. The more you know about his life, the more you realize that courage really is, as Hemingway put it, the ability to maintain grace under pressure.

Tucker was in first grade when he first actually realized the way many others looked at him. Because his parents had always allowed him to do whatever he could manage, because he was never given any special treatment, he had never thought of himself as really different.

But that changed one Halloween when he was dressed from head to toe in a Sylvester the Cat costume, with even his hands covered. When he walked down the hallway of Sutton Elementary School in southwest Houston, one child after another yelled out, "Nice costume, Tucker. That's a great costume, Tuck." Teachers did the same. Finally, Tucker asked a third-grader how everyone knew who he was.

The boy laughed. "Oh, come on. You're the cripple. Everyone knows that. You know how stupid you walk. And you run like a chicken."

The mask covered Tucker's tears. For the rest of the day all he could hear was the boy laughing, calling him a cripple. Tucker tried to run home from school faster than he ever had before. He wondered if everybody who saw him thought he looked like a chicken. He fell so many times on the way home that he tore up his costume.

"Mom, they said I'm a cripple," he said, sobbing as he opened the door to his home. "Am I a cripple?"

Tucker's mother got out a dictionary. She read to her son. "Cripple: to make unable or unfit to act, function effectively, etc." And then she began to ask him questions. Can't you walk to school? Can't you ride a bike? Can't you operate a skateboard? Can't you swim in the swimming pool? Can't you play baseball? On and on the questions went. Tucker answered yes to every question.

"It seems to me you're not crippled, Tucker," Judi Church said. "You just do things in ways that look different because of cerebral palsy. We've always told you that."

The mother then told her seven-year-old son that all people are different in some way and that anyone who says someone's crippled because of that difference is either mean or not too bright. Some of us are better at running or jumping or playing cards or doing arithmetic than others are, but that doesn't mean that those who can't do them as well are crippled. Tucker knew what his mother meant and he hugged and kissed her. But he also knew what the boy at school meant when he called him a cripple. He had walked in front of the mirror. The way he moved did look strange.

Tucker never told his mother and father how much that first reference to him being a cripple affected him as he grew older. That didn't seem like being a man, and, besides, he didn't want to worry them as his older sister did. No doubt because it was the first time he realized the way many people saw him, the first-grade episode had even more hurtful staying power than other youngsters' periodic imitations of his walk. The scene would replay in his mind when he wanted to talk to a girl, and then he ended up being too afraid to talk to her. Would a pretty girl want to be around someone who looked stupid? Who wants to be around someone who runs like a chicken? (Only recently has Tucker realized that he probably became the class clown in school because he didn't want people to think a cripple couldn't have fun. Hey, he could be funnier than anyone else.)

Had it not been for his frequent visits to the home of his friends, Chris and Brad Parsell, the Halloween incident may have had much more of a paralyzing impact. The boys' parents, Randy and Brenda Parsell, are both legally blind. He's a piano tuner and she's a certified Braille transcriber. She can see an image on the TV screen if she's a couple of inches from it. Nobody doubts Randy when he says he can hear a pin drop.

The way they have dealt with blindness has helped

Tucker see how life should be lived. He liked their idea of putting bells on children and pets so they'd know where they were. He told his mother that if he ever had children he'd do the same thing. "You can't always see where your kids are," Tucker said.

There were days when Tucker would go to the Parsells' home and do little more than sit around. No one knew at the time that he was getting an inspiration fix. He says now that he wasn't even conscious of what he was doing. He'd listen as Brenda sang, watch as she vacuumed the living room, cooked in the kitchen, kissed her boys. He'd hear Randy talk about a joke he had heard at work, about the problems of tuning Yamaha and Steinway grands. They were parents who wanted to know their sons' batting and grade-point averages and parents who believed all children should eat vegetables. They were homeowners who made sure their lawn was cut each week. Yes, they did it themselves. They had the steps down pat on how far to go each way across the lawn. Brenda loved to plant flowers, always making sure she planted the most fragrant. She loved to pick her own roses and have them in her house. The Parsells talked about electricity rates going up and they told their sons they had to go easy on the air conditioning. They wondered if the Astros would ever win a pennant, if the Houston Oilers would ever win a Super Bowl, if the Houston Rockets would ever win an NBA Championship.

The picture Tucker saw was that of everyday people doing everyday things. Blind, yes; crippled, no.

There were days when Brenda and Randy got on one of those four-wheel bikes you see at the beach and they pedaled all over the neighborhood. They'd ride near the curb, with Brad and Chris riding their bikes next to them. Everyday people doing everyday things. Many days the Parsells walked up to the park to watch their boys play baseball. They knew just where to turn, how many steps to take.

When the Parsells got to the ballpark—their son, Chris, played on the same team as Tucker for years—they often sat in the stands with Judi and Terry Church. Terry always let them know what Chris was doing. If he told them that Chris was upset after missing a ground ball, both Brenda and Randy would yell, "Keep your head up, Son."

They'd hear the ball meet the bat and ask Terry if it was time to cheer or boo. They'd shout to Chris and his teammates to keep their eyes on the ball. Sometimes, they'd even lead other fans in singing, "Take me out to the ballgame... "

Win or lose, the smiles of Brenda and Randy were so broad that Tucker often wondered if their faces could break.

"I never talked to them about how important they were to me," Tucker says. "They were never feeling sorry for themselves. It was so incredible to me. I wondered how they did it. I guess I still do. I tried putting a blindfold on and seeing if I could get around and I couldn't do it. I suppose with practice I could. It makes me think people can do just about anything if they put their minds to it. Knowing them inspired me, for sure. I didn't realize until I got older how much they inspired me. A lot of time when I felt bad I remembered how they could be happy and not even see. They made me realize I shouldn't focus on what I can't do."

The elder Parsells, who hadn't known what an impression they had made on Tucker, were delighted at the news. "So that's why he was always coming by here, for inspiration," Brenda Parsell says, laughing as she sat in the living room of her spotless home.

You are struck right away by Brenda Parsell's *joie de vivre*. When she says it's a beautiful day, you get the feeling that practically every day is beautiful to her. Entrants in beauty pageants try to force her kind of spark. But she's there smiling, remembering Tucker saying, "Hi, Mrs. Parsells, you going to come watch the Little League game tonight?" And she sighs. Tucker was, in her estimation, innocence at its grandest, manners at their best. Always please and thank you. Always asking if it was okay if her boys came out to play. Always telling her how nice the lawn looked, how good her food was. When she says she misses seeing him, having him around, you know its true.

Not once in the twelve years that they talked regularly with Tucker did the elder Parsells ever bring up the subject of disabilities. "What I always liked about Tucker's parents is their willingness to let him be independent," Brenda Parsells says. "My parents were like that. If Randy and I reinforced the fact that Tucker shouldn't dwell on his difficulties, then that makes me feel very good."

Why anyone would focus on what they can't do is beyond Brenda Parsells. At the thought of people suggesting that this job or that sport is beyond somebody unless it truly is, irks her. The frustration seeps out. "We can't waste potential in America," she said. "No more. I didn't want Tucker to ever think he couldn't be whatever."

Tucker's parents realized early on he wasn't like Paige, a sister eight years older who also had cerebral palsy. When she found she couldn't get around just like other children, she wanted to stay inside the house all the time. She'd play with dolls or jacks, do anything to stay away from other kids' innocent questions about why she walked as she did. Strange as it may seem, her discipline for acting up was to be sent outside to play. She was so withdrawn that they worried constantly about what would become of her. Tucker was a different case altogether. After he started walking at age three, he didn't let the fact that he couldn't fully control his motor function slow down his interaction with other children. Tucker's friends and former neighbors of the Churches remember that, unlike Paige, he was always in the thick of everything.

"I was always amazed by his heart," says Kay Durrett, who used to live down the street from the Churches. "I can remember when the boys in the neighborhood would all be out on skateboards and Tucker would be there, too.

But he had to be on his stomach, pushing with his hands, because he couldn't balance well enough to stand up. It didn't seem to bother him at all. He'd be laughing and carrying on just like everybody else. And he seemed to be able to go just as fast that way. I'd get tears in my eyes watching it."

Joe Lyons, who's been a friend of Tucker's since before kindergarten, recalls that Tucker would fall repeatedly when they played kickball or roller-skated or played hide-and-seek. They played for hours on end, Tucker often coming away with torn pants and skinned elbows.

"But he never let any of that bother him," Lyons says. "He'd just keep coming even though it always seemed like he'd have to get stitches in his chin. When some of the kids asked him why he walked and ran like he did, he'd just say he had cerebral palsy. Those questions didn't bother him at all when he was small. He acted like it was no big deal, so we did too. We didn't know what cerebral palsy was then, but he was having fun and always playing with us so nobody cared. He just got around a little differently and all the guys accepted it."

The Sharpstown section of Houston was where the Churches had moved to from Connecticut in 1978. It was then an ideal place for a youngster to grow up. Planned and partially built in the 1950s by developer Frank Sharp, the development of twenty-five thousand homes on sixty-five hundred acres was aimed at middle-class home buyers with a myriad of recreational interests.

In 1971, the Securities & Exchange Commission filed suit against Sharp, accusing him and many top state officials of stock manipulation, but the shock of this event and the deterioration of the area didn't seem to be in the picture then for the Church family.

The Churches knew nothing of the scandal that preceded them when they arrived in the area. All they knew was that Sharpstown seemed like a clean and safe place. Street crime had yet to be a major concern when the Churches put down their roots. There was a sense of community, tidiness, and safety that allowed children to come and go as they pleased. The tree-lined streets gave the area a small town feel. No one thought anything of Tucker and his friends playing kickball at night under a street light.

Today, however, Sharpstown's sense of security has been at least partially replaced by the blight of urban chaos and neglect. Parents worry about letting their children out in the daytime, let alone at night. Even the mall sometimes becomes infested with gang members. That's why the Churches moved to Alvin, a small town outside of Houston, two years ago. While many pillars of the middle class still reside in Sharpstown, others have moved, often leasing their homes when they can't sell them for a fair price. Apartments offering cheap rent in the area are often used as crack houses. The sound of gunfire is not uncommon. In 1992, a six-year-old child, David Kazmouz, who grew up two streets behind the former Church home, was kidnapped from in front of his house. Nearly a year later, the remains of his body were found miles away in a heavily wooded area. His photograph had been on billboards as far away as Los Angeles and New York City.

For Tucker, though, Sharpstown wasn't about kidnappings or gunfire or the drug trade. And it wasn't about falling while riding bikes with Joe and Frank Lyons, or about tossing a football wildly with Orlando and Filiberto Martinez, or about lying on his stomach while skateboarding with Christopher and Brad Parsell. To Tucker, Sharpstown was mainly about playing baseball with all of them.

Five minutes from his Carvel Lane home sat Bayland Park. There are baseball fields there, it seems, as far as the eye can see. He'd walk or ride his bike over with friends and before he knew it, a rush of delight would have zipped through him. He was as much a part of the action as they were.

Sometimes he'd ride over by himself and practice running around the bases, to see how fast he could run without tripping. He'd practice sliding, too, sometimes tearing his pants so his mother would get upset. But she'd only be upset for a little while, until he told her how he'd done it.

Other organized sports—soccer, football, basketball—wouldn't work for him. He couldn't run well enough for soccer. He'd drag the toes of his shoes on the ground and could never get a foot around to launch a decent kick. Even without soccer, his foot dragging generally meant he needed at least one new pair of shoes every month. Two weeks after he got a pair of shoes, you could see where his socks covered his big toes. Every time he'd try to kick the soccer ball it seemed he'd end up on his face. He had had ten stitches in his chin to prove it.

His mother always said he was too small to make a football team, that the players would end up using him as the ball. One time he had tried to play and had been caught under the pile. He couldn't breathe. He was sure he had been crushed to death. As for basketball, the running and jumping and quick changing of directions made it pretty much impossible for someone who dragged his feet. Besides, trying to throw a ball accurately more than ten feet in the air when your arm won't straighten out tends to become frustrating.

Not being able to join soccer or football or basketball teams with his friends hurt, but it didn't eat at him. He had baseball. He didn't play well, but he was passable. He couldn't hit the ball hard or throw the ball far or run the bases fast, but he did all of them well enough to compete. Best of all, he was with his buddies. He was part of the whole, the team. His friends wanted him on the team because he was the guy who never stopped yelling encouragement. He made them feel good. From the warm-up to the last pitch, he chattered:

"Hit it out of here!"

"Show us what you can do."

"Smoke it by him."

"He couldn't hit the broadside of a barn!"

Once in a pickup game when he was eight years old, Tucker was the first player chosen. Not because he was the best player, but because he was the best talker. The boy who was captain made his choice, he said, because his dad had told him that team morale and spirit are key elements in having a winning team. That's why Tucker was chosen first—to fire up the team. The scene never left him. From that day forward, he realized he had an important role to play on any team.

Even today, as he helps coach his little brother Josh's team, Tucker is the one who can always be heard. Fire the kids up, make them have confidence in themselves, and they'll play better, he says. "Come on, Josh, be a man," he says as his brother waits on a pitch.

Tucker says his greatest moment in organized baseball came when he was eight years old. The memory always carries with it his first real sense of accomplishment. Tucker, now a high-school junior, smiles and then closes his eyes as he recounts the first time he reached home plate after hitting a ball.

He relishes telling the story. Sometimes he tells it with humor. Other times with a tear in his eye. If you get a group of war veterans together, you often see the same kind of emotional tug of war as they recall their time in harm's way. For Tucker, Little League became a test of his manhood, his big opportunity for camaraderie, his chance to sacrifice for a larger cause, the good of the team.

"It was my second year in Little League and I was on the Rams when I hit a ball and it rolled right up the third base line. I was running to first and I tripped and fell down but they overthrew the first base man so I got to first safe. Then I started running to second because they were still running after the ball. I had never even seen second base before when I was hitting. They got the ball and threw it to second and it rolled right between the second baseman's legs. So I started running to third and all the time I couldn't believe it. Third base! The second baseman threw it to the third baseman and there must have been a hole in his glove because the ball went right through him. So I ran home. When I slid in safe, my mom was yelling and screaming and my coach was crying. Players from both sides came out to congratulate me. Everybody was yelling. Oh, man, I had seen something like that happening in my mind so many times. It was the greatest feeling. Ever since then I've thought just about anything in life is possible. I figured if I could get a home run, I could do anything."

It's almost as if the British sportswriter Brian Glanville had been writing about Tucker when he made his insightful observation about the importance of athletics:

"They demonstrate the scope of human possibility, which is unlimited. The inconceivable is conceived, and then it is accomplished."

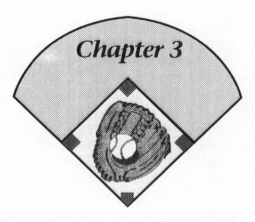

Chapter 3

We're in the family room of the Church's ranch-style house in Alvin, a rural community forty miles south of Houston, a place best known as the home of record-breaking pitcher Nolan Ryan. Outside, Tucker's parents sit under an oak tree with their son Josh and visit with daughters Edythe and April, who live just down the blacktop road with their husbands and children. An inviting above-ground swimming pool, with fresh landscaping all around, stands ready for use. So does the trampoline on which overly rambunctious Tucker broke his foot.

The laughter filtering through the closed windows makes it difficult to hear Tucker. He gets up from the couch to look outside. He is nine inches taller than he was three years ago. He and his family credit the operations on his legs and feet at the Shriners Hospital in Houston for that. Always soft-spoken, he is particularly so as he talks about how he has been ridiculed. He still finds it hard to believe that other people sometimes come up beside him and imitate his walk. "They're weird," he says with a shrug. "What else can I say? They just don't know any better."

The older he gets, the more Tucker figures he somehow inherited his parents' strength. Few couples could have endured so much without either divorcing or ending up in an asylum. Watching them holding hands under the oak tree, it's hard to believe they have ever had a care in the world. Judi's now a short-haired blond who loves to laugh. You can hear it, you're sure, a block away. Terry's as quiet as Judi is outgoing.

Their courtship never provided any foreshadowing of the misfortunes to come. The first meeting of Terry Church and Judi Jacquin in 1963 sounds as though it was dreamed up by a filmmaker in the ever-romantic Hollywood of the fifties. Terry, a slim, muscular submariner, had left his base in New London, Connecticut, to ogle women as they walked down the boardwalk in Asbury Park, New Jersey. A resident of nearby Maplewood, Judi, a natural blond, showed up with her six-year-old cousin Suzie for an afternoon of fun on amusement rides. There wasn't a cloud in the sky on that warm August day and there was just enough breeze off the ocean to make it pleasant. The sailor said to the tall blond: "You know, I have a niece about this little girl's age. I really miss her. Why don't you let me show you both a good time?"

And you thought lines like that only worked in movies!

As they watched Suzie ride the merry-go-round, the pair talked about how much they'd both love a large family. (Honest. No scriptwriter would dare write such a scene for a couple's first meeting.) Eight would be enough, they said. An only child, eighteen-year-old Judi had dreamed of a house full of kids. When the sailor from Pittsburgh—a guy who didn't go nuts staying underwater for more than a month—said the more kids the better, she glowed. Judi was impressed enough with Terry to call off her engagement to her high-school sweetheart a few days later.

Judi, then working as a bank teller, found herself bubbling with life again, just as she had before her mother had died a year earlier. Every weekend when her sailor wasn't at sea, he'd drive to New Jersey from Connecticut and they'd talk about their future, about starting up a kind of modern-day Waltons family together. He couldn't wait to play baseball with their boys, take them hunting and fishing. After Terry promised her father, a retired welder for Union Carbide, that he wouldn't make a career of the navy, she had her dad's blessing. "If you're going to have all those kids, you better be home with them," her father told Terry.

They married in Prospect Presbyterian Church in Maplewood, New Jersey, on September 19, 1964, a little more than a year after they had met. Even when her father accidentally stepped on the train of her dress and tore off the lovely lace as she walked down the aisle, the smile didn't come off Judi's face. Her dream was coming true. Lace doesn't bring you a big, happy family. A good man does.

They moved to Maryland, where Terry worked for an air-conditioning company. Nine months and ten days after they married, Edythe was born. Perfect Edythe. Gorgeous Edythe. Life, the Churches thought, is so easy if you have a plan. Only seven beautiful babies to go before they found heaven on earth.

Edythe's behavior seemed to follow what the baby books indicated she should be doing at her age level. At sixteen weeks she liked to be on the big bed, and loved to be held. Her eyes would glisten and her face would break into a smile as she was lifted into the sitting position. Judi would hum "Rock-a-bye-baby," and Edythe would react as though she had heard the most beautiful voice on earth. She cooed, chuckled, laughed aloud. She'd smile back when she was smiled at. Terry would hold a paper in his hand and make an arc and Edythe would follow it with her eyes. At twenty-eight weeks, Edythe was picking up rattles in her little hands. Sometimes she'd suck her own toes. Now she loved to hear Terry's low voice, which had startled her before. At forty weeks, she would melt Terry's heart by saying, "Da-Da." And she looked so cute playing pat-a-cake. At one year she walked and loved to play peek-a-boo. The Churches couldn't wait to have more children.

Not in their worst nightmares did they ever envision what would happen in the next three years. Two more children, Paige and April, were born two years apart—

both several weeks premature, both with problems so severe that the doctors didn't think they'd survive. Judi, who couldn't believe she was doing it, had an abortion when she became pregnant again. The Churches were so unnerved they decided to have no more children.

If their dream hadn't died, it was in a deep coma.

During Judi's pregnancy with Edythe, a doctor told her she and Terry had an Rh blood type incompatibility that could cause a future pregnancy to result in a premature birth. (At that time, the Rogam immunization to correct such a problem, was not widely available.)

"We were young and naive and didn't ask all the questions about what an Rh incompatibility could mean," Judi says. "Plus, when we looked at Edythe, she was just so perfect."

Paige, born six weeks early and weighing only three pounds at birth, didn't come home from the hospital for two months. When she did, she screamed day and night, as though someone was stabbing a knife in her. She never relaxed. Her hands were always clenched, her tiny feet always rigid, pointed inward. Alarmed, the Churches took her to one doctor after another. The doctors told them to relax, that premature infants are slow to develop.

When Paige was two years old, Terry's mother took her to a hospital in Pittsburgh, where doctors diagnosed her as retarded, with little time to live. The Churches were crushed. That same night Judi received a phone call from another hospital: Her father had died in New Jersey.

The next day there was more news. Judi was pregnant again. "I know it seems strange," Judi says, "but we didn't fear it. We just didn't think any more bad things could happen. We weren't keying in on our blood."

The Churches decided to live in Judi's hometown. Terry opened up his own home repair business. A New Jersey neurologist tested Paige and found that she wasn't retarded, but did have other symptoms of cerebral palsy—movement problems. To the Churches, that was good news. She would be able to think! She wasn't dying! They read all they could about cerebral palsy and found that it's a condition caused by damage to the brain during pregnancy, labor, or shortly following birth. "Cerebral" refers to the brain and "palsy" to a disorder of movement or posture.

As the book *Children With Cerebral Palsy* suggests, there have probably been children with cerebral palsy as long as there have been children. But doctors didn't begin to study it specifically as a condition until 1861, the year the English physician Dr. William John Little published a paper outlining the neurological problems of children with spastic diplegia. (Diplegia means cerebral palsy that largely affects a child's legs. Because of spastic leg muscles, children with diplegia generally stand on their toes and scissor their legs.)

It wasn't until the late 1800s that the term "cerebral palsy" was coined by the British doctor William Osler. Some of the first-known papers on the condition were written by Dr. Sigmund Freud, best known for his work in psychiatry.

In the past, children with cerebral palsy were often separated from their families at an early age, and institutionalized. Or kept in a back room or basement. They were outcasts, mistakes to be hidden away just like those with mental disorders. Opportunities for their enjoyment, education, or employment were slim or none. Fortunately, in the last few decades attitudes have changed.

Like Tucker, Paige is one of the estimated seven hundred thousand children and adults in the United States with cerebral palsy. According to the United Cerebral Palsy Association, each year an estimated ten thousand babies are born with cerebral palsy or acquire it early in life. It is the most widespread lifetime disability in the nation, but it is neither progressive nor communicable. Among the causes of the condition are premature birth and Rh and A-B-O blood-type incompatibility between parents. Depending on which part of the brain has been damaged and the degree of involvement of the central nervous system, a person may manifest one or more of the symptoms of cerebral palsy—increased or decreased muscle tone, spasms, involuntary movement, disturbance in gait and mobility, abnormal sensation and perception, impairment of sight, hearing, or speech, and mental retardation.

The unusual irritability and tenseness Paige displayed as an infant, coupled with her difficulty in sucking from a bottle, should have suggested to doctors early on that she had cerebral palsy. Earlier treatment of the condition with medications could have at least made the first two years of life more comfortable for both her and her parents. She did eventually get braces and have surgery on her legs and feet to improve her coordination and to correct the deformities, but her walk is still severely impaired.

As the Churches settled into a routine of taking Paige to a cerebral palsy center, April was born. It was 1968. She, too, was eight weeks premature. Eight exchange transfusions were done to try and prevent the onset of cerebral palsy. While she had seizures, no other symptoms of the condition appeared. The Grand Mal seizures, however, were terrifying. With seemingly no notice, her muscles would stiffen and she'd fall to the floor, unconscious. Later, her limbs would jerk rhythmically. The spasms often lasted for several minutes, and the Churches would lay April on her side and make her as comfortable as possible. But often, she had trouble breathing, and she'd lose bladder control. When the spasms ended, she'd be exhausted and fall into a deep sleep. Almost always, the Churches would take her to the emergency room to make sure no serious damage had been done. Doctors finally prescribed phenobarbital and dilantin, and her seizures became infrequent. And by the age of five, she stopped having them altogether.

In any household where there's three small children,

there is always a ton of work, tumult, and tension. Wash the clothes, warm the bottles, change the diapers, cook the food, wipe the noses, comfort the sick—virtually non-stop, everyday domestic action. It's hard to imagine, however, what it was like in the Church's small, three-bedroom home when two of the three children were having severe problems. Always, it seemed, Paige cried.

Living now in Japan with her serviceman husband and two young children, Paige has no idea how her parents coped. "My two kids are normal and I find it an incredible strain. I don't think I could have ever done what they've done and stayed sane."

Even after Paige outgrew the constant irritability, the commonplace seemed a distant dream. When other three-year-olds toddled about, Paige pulled herself across the floor or ground much like an infantryman under fire.

Unable to walk until the age of four, and then only with the aid of crutches, she cried herself to sleep every night after her parents placed her in the braces that doctors thought might straighten her legs. "Oh, did they hurt!" Paige says today.

The crying at bedtime took its toll on Judi and Terry Church. What had been a wonderful time with Edythe wasn't like that at all with Paige. She knew bedtime meant the braces that would immobilize her. So she cried.

It didn't matter if they read her stories or not. She cried.

Her parents felt that she saw them as the enemy.

"Bedtime was a sad time instead of a fun, close time, and it was that way for years," Terry Church said. "The doctors said it was the right thing to do, but it was hell."

On top of Paige's difficulties, the Churches were dealing with April's problems too. April had as many as five terrifying seizures each day. She would fall to the floor, her eyes would roll back in her head, and she would shake violently and void before falling into a deep thirty-minute sleep.

For awhile, every minute of every day Judi felt like crying. But the only place she felt comfortable doing it was in the shower, where Terry and the children wouldn't hear her, where she wouldn't upset them. Day after day, she'd stand there and weep, sometimes dropping to her knees as the water sprayed over her, as the questions whirled round in her head.

Why did this have to happen to the babies? Will they ever be able to marry and have children of their own?

She'd blame herself for what was happening to her children. "All I wanted to be was a good mother," she'd cry. She'd beg God for help. She'd hear a voice and think someone was calling. But then she would realize she was only hearing the echo of her own anguish.

There was no money for baby sitters, no relatives to help out. If she wanted to go to the grocery store, all three children had to go with her. Judi had no close friends. She had no time to make them. At that time, Terry worked in maintenance for a small, Shorehills, New Jersey, firm and went to college at night so he could earn an engineering degree. The growing family was sorely in need of funds that a job with more training would bring, so Judi was supportive. But she had to bear a lot of the emotional load of the family alone. Often when Terry got home, Judi excused herself and headed straight for her self-prescribed shower therapy.

Compounding Judi's emotional torment was the pain that often shot through her from a slipped disk. While pregnant with April, Judi had felt something give in her lower back. Carrying Paige, who was wearing heavy braces, had been too much. She began to wear a back brace. Sometimes it helped, often it didn't. Over the next several years, there would be times when she couldn't get out of bed and Edythe would have to cook and care for the other children. It took ten years for Judi to work up the courage to have a back operation. This was largely because Judi's mother had died during an operation on her back when Judi was just a little girl. Her heart had simply stopped.

Judi didn't know how her children could survive without a mother.

The strain on Judi and Terry became practically unbearable in 1970 when Judi learned she was pregnant again. The children—Edythe, four; Paige, three; and April, two—often asked Judi why she was crying. "Emotionally and financially, Terry and I were both strung out," Judi says.

Terry argued that there was no way they could handle another child that might well have problems. He wanted her to have an abortion. Finally, just before it would have no longer been possible, she did. She was hysterical throughout the procedure in a New York City hospital. What about the big family she had planned to have? What if the baby had turned out like Edythe? Or even if it had turned out like Paige and April, weren't they going to be okay? What about the pain the unborn child had suffered? She went home in a daze, moving amidst her shattered dreams—the promise of what might have been, what should have been. She felt as if a vital part of her life had been destroyed.

For several months she made life hell on earth for Terry. Crying in the shower no longer helped her get her head straight. She yelled. She screamed. She threw things. If he said it was a nice day, she said it was a lousy day. She blamed him for the abortion and blamed herself for being so wishy-washy. She was miserable and she was intent on making everyone else miserable. Finally, Terry moved out.

Only for a few days, but he left.

When he returned, they talked things out. It was then, late at night at the kitchen table, that they mapped the strategy that has served them and their children well.

In the book *After the Tears, Parents Talk About Raising a Child With a Disability*, author Robin Simons says the worst kind of marital stress can't be avoided when the dream of a normal child is dashed. Judi Church says Simons knows what she's talking about.

In the Churches' relationship, Judi wanted to talk about her hurt. Terry wanted to keep it inside.

But as the Churches sat there late into the night, they decided they weren't going to look back. They decided that only pain could come from dwelling on mistakes in the past, on what might have been. Should'a, would'a, could'a wasn't going to be included in their conversations. They would be eradicated from their vocabularies. They were going to make as much of life as they could for themselves and their children. They were good people who hadn't been dealt the best hand, but that didn't mean they had to fold. They couldn't give up. They owed it to their children to give them the best life they could.

For Judi, the abortion was a turning point. She became far more independent. If anything, her love for Terry was greater than ever, but she knew she needed to stand on her own two feet. She saw the way life was going to be—her running the family while Terry worked outside the home—and that didn't bother her. They had enough money, good insurance. What did bother her is that she hadn't taken more control over decisions, asking what should be done when it should have been her call.

In the final analysis, she decided that only you are in control of you—nobody else. The sooner you realize that, the less complicated life is to live. Never again would she do something that she didn't completely concur with. She'd let her conscience be her guide. It was this mind-set that lead her to fight Little League on behalf of Tucker. Having that baby taken away from her had given her strength she didn't know she had.

In 1973, after Terry and Judi had come to peace with their lives, they consulted with doctors and decided to try for a boy of their own. Doctors said the RhoGAM (Rh Immune Globulin) immunization wouldn't work on her, but the Churches were assured that if there were problems, exchange transfusions were the answer.

The desire for more children couldn't have been stronger. Edythe was fine. So, incredibly, was April. Paige was doing better with therapy. Their dream of a modern-day Waltons family still lived. Besides, Terry now had a good job as the maintenance engineer with a prestigious nursing home in New York City. And with advanced medical techniques and the best prenatal care, the Churches felt sure they could have a healthy baby. Despite careful monitoring of her pregnancy by a team of doctors—the baby seemed fine during an amniocentesis—Judi went into labor seven weeks early. Terry had already gone to work, so Judi climbed into her Ford station wagon and drove the forty miles to New York City herself. Terry met her at the hospital. An hour after Judi arrived there on March 4, 1974, she delivered the baby that would later become known as Tucker Church.

The doctor's report was grim. The baby's lungs were hardly developed and the infant was having difficulty breathing. There was a heart defect and jaundice.

Even with exchange transfusions, the baby's chances of survival were slim.

As Judi lay in the hospital a couple of days later, a doctor called Terry at home. He said the baby was dying and there needed to be a name on the birth certificate, so the hospital would have a name to put on the death certificate. Distraught, Terry could only think of the name that a neighbor had suggested—Eric. He didn't like the name, but it didn't really matter. His son was going to die anyway.

Eric Church came home two months later.

Judi disliked the name Eric even more than her husband did. They don't know why.

When Judi heard what Terry had named the child, she said, "Uck." And that's what the baby was called until Richard, a two-year-old foster child living with the Churches, said "Tucker" instead of "Uck." Four years later, when the Churches moved to Houston, they had their son's name legally changed to Tucker.

(Truth is definitely stranger than fiction.)

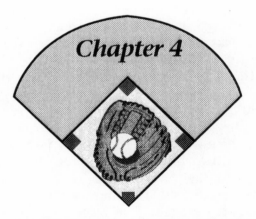

Chapter 4

At the age of nine months, Tucker was diagnosed as having cerebral palsy. In her heart, Judi had known it well before then. Like Paige before him, Tucker had his tight hands always balled in a fist. His toes were also always tight. Even in the bathtub he didn't relax.

Edythe, who was nine when Tucker came home from the hospital, would often hear him crying in the night and take him a bottle. "My parents were so exhausted I'd hear him first," she said. "He couldn't suck well because of the cerebral palsy and he'd need a bottle every hour or two. I'd change a lot of diapers at night, too."

Tucker sometimes refers to Edythe as "my second mother." And in many ways she took on those duties, especially as the condition of Judi's back deteriorated. While her mother lay in bed in traction, ten-year-old Edythe made sandwiches for lunches and cooked up hamburger dinners. When a next-door-neighbor's boy picked on her sister Paige, Edythe went to talk to the boy. She ended up with a black eye.

Later, as a teenager, Edythe rebelled at having to baby-sit so much. Her mother sees it as natural now, but at the time it seemed not so natural. When you're in a life crisis, it's hard to see the whole picture. So Judi wasn't happy when Edythe moved in with other relatives for awhile.

Edythe loved her brothers and sisters, but she wanted to be, well, a teenager, too. Not just a second mother. Dates, dances, football games would be fun. What other kids saw as normal.

"It wore on me, baby-sitting so much," Edythe says. "My mother was an only child, so she didn't realize what it was like to just basically do that."

When the family lived in Bridgeport, Connecticut, Tucker was sent to the cerebral palsy center every day for therapy. He didn't sit up until he was eighteen months old. Then Terry constructed some short parallel bars so he could practice walking. Judi and Edythe tried another technique. To help him, they'd sit him up against the refrigerator and say, "walk!" and Tucker would try to walk across the kitchen. He'd take a step and fall, but he'd giggle and try again. The more steps he took, the more applause he received. He aimed to please. It was difficult to get him to stop trying. He finally walked when he was three-and-a-half years old.

While Tucker didn't have the best balance in the world, the biggest problem he had with walking came from a goat. For some reason she still can't explain, Judi had always wanted a goat. So Terry got her one. There were seven acres of land with the house they were renting so you'd think that there would have been enough room for a family of five and a goat. But this ol' goat—fortunately, it didn't have any horns—loved to tackle people. Especially Tucker. The goat would come up behind Tucker and knock him down as easily as a bowling ball takes out pins. Finally, Terry came up with a plan for Tucker's defense. He bought him a rubber mallet and told his son to hit the goat between the eyes with it the next time he was tackled.

The plan worked. Tucker gave the goat a couple of whacks and that was that. The goat didn't get anything but his feelings hurt and from then on Tucker was able to walk around the grounds in peace.

His sisters always knew where he was. He seemed to be always laughing.

Though Tucker's disposition was positive, he had frequent bouts of colds, followed by pneumonia. In children with cerebral palsy, colds often drag on and on. And this was not just in the winter, when he loved to go sledding. Tucker got pneumonia in the summer, too. Pneumonia is the most common cause of death in children with cerebral palsy, so doctors recommended that the family move to a warmer climate. The move wasn't made right away because Judi was pregnant again. "It definitely wasn't planned," she says. "But I couldn't go through another abortion."

Marriah was born prematurely in 1978. Her intrauterine transfusions worked. She didn't get cerebral palsy.

Maybe things were really going to start looking up.

The Churches' move to Houston in 1978 turned out to be just what the doctor ordered. Tucker's health improved immediately. For the first time, he didn't have trouble breathing. Yes, things were definitely looking up.

Terry took an engineering job with the Shamrock Hilton. The family soon flourished in what was then the nation's fastest growing city.

The Arab oil embargo that fueled the recession in the rest of the country had only spawned faster growth in a city where the dominant industries fed off Texas' energy resources. During the seventies, nearly one million people moved to the six-county Houston region. Houston natives, an increasingly rare species, would tell the Churches they fully appreciated what Gen. George Custer had meant at Little Big Horn when he asked, "Where did all these Indians come from?"

That drawling, tongue-in-cheek humor—brought on by the onslaught of "American foreigners" escaping depressed economies, was delivered with the winking, macho assurance that one thousand new immigrants a week couldn't fire a fatal arrow into their sprawling, boom-town metropolis.

For all the talk of oil, Terry, with his penchant for science, also figured that the aerospace industry had had a lot to do with the city's phenomenal growth after 1960. He was right. Becoming the home of the nation's space center in September 1961 gave the city a virtual booster-rocket ride toward the twenty-first century. Houston was fortunate to have friends in high places when it came time to pick the site of the space station. When President Kennedy challenged the United States to be the first nation to put men on the moon, Lyndon Johnson, a former speech teacher at Sam Houston High School, was Vice President. And Texas Congressman Albert Thomas was chairman of the House subcommittee that controlled the National Aeronautics & Space Administration's (NASA) purse strings. When Thomas learned that NASA was looking for a site on which to locate a manned spacecraft training and mission center, he didn't have to bend too many arms to bring the selection team to Houston. President Kennedy spent the last evening of his life at a Houston testimonial dinner for Thomas.

This was the Churches' kind of town, a place with a positive attitude toward getting on with it. They were floored when they learned that Houston is actually fifty-five miles from the Gulf of Mexico, but that its leaders had had the vision to dredge a channel to the ocean—a move that made Houston the nation's third largest port in terms of total tonnage and the leader in foreign trade tonnage.

The energy of the city seemed to rub off on the Church family, who found it a city of hope. For seven years it was utopia. If it was good enough for men who flew through the sky to see the stars up close and personal, for astronauts like the heroic Alan Shepard, it was good enough for them. When they found out that thousands of Americans came to Houston to receive treatment at M.D. Anderson Hospital for supposedly incurable cancers, they weren't surprised. "Can't" didn't seem to be in anyone's vocabulary.

Houston was home to heart transplant kings Dr. Denton Cooley and Dr. Michael DeBakey.

That was the kind of place it seemed to be. If one thing didn't work, you just had to try something else. The Churches had never sensed so much energy before. Or fun either.

With his family in good spirits, the city's outrageous traffic didn't bother Terry. Bumper to bumper traffic for twenty miles—no problem. Even Paige had started to get out of the house more. All of the children were doing well in school. Friends of the Church children always seemed to be around. Some days, Edythe would look outside and count twenty-five bikes on the lawn. One kid after another would eat with them. They'd serve themselves, say what a wonderful mom Tucker had, and eat some more. Judi loved it. The more kids around, the better.

Terry took an even better engineering job at Hermann Hospital, where he still works today. As for Tucker, well, if he wasn't at home, he always seemed to be at the baseball field. Little League coaches loved his chatter. So did the other kids. Talk about spirit! He had enough for the whole team.

His friend Joe Lyons is still in awe of Tucker's love for baseball. "It was like an addiction," he says. "He wouldn't stop talking about baseball."

Neighbor Kate Durrett remembers Tucker for organizing games for youngsters, and for his patience. Her seven-year-old son Joel was embarrassed that he couldn't ride a bike, so Tucker took him aside one day and told him he'd teach him. "For the next two hours, he ran up and down the street behind Joel with his twisted legs going this way and that," Joel's mother says. "Tucker would fall while he was chasing Joel, but he'd get up laughing and he wouldn't give up until Joel learned how to ride a bike. My husband and I couldn't teach Joel, but Tucker did."

Neighbor Dora Martinez enjoyed Tucker's upbeat and polite manner.

"He just never seemed to think he had a problem," she recalls. "For the longest time, he seemed to be all smiles. When he saw me or my husband, he'd always wave."

But in the sixth grade, the year Tucker turned twelve, things changed radically. It was as though a gremlin had crept into Tucker's room one night and yanked his feel-good switch into the off position. Under the best of circumstances, the shift from elementary to middle school is difficult, but it was then that Tucker realized his cerebral palsy could hold him back in his studies—not what you want to learn when you're trying to make up for a lack of brawn with an acrobatic mind.

Tucker found that he didn't have the dexterity to write quickly enough to keep up with the more demanding pace of middle school. The teacher would be talking about battles in World War II and he'd still be writing about the first one she mentioned, while she was talking about the fifth. Surprisingly, no teachers picked up on his problem and he was too proud to admit it to anyone, a fact that he rues today. His grades plummeted and overnight, it seemed, he developed a who-gives-a-damn attitude.

He became known in school as the guy who always cracked jokes in math and English class. He started hanging out with guys who smoked. Tough guys. He thought they'd be protective of him when people imitated his walk. They weren't.

Joe Lyons remembers that at Jane Long Middle School there were often students who would mock Tucker's gait. Tucker wanted to fight, but he was so small other students would just push him aside. Once he did knock the wind out of one jerk's stomach. Unfortunately, the jerk got up and gave him a whack that sent him flying. So Joe Lyons, a six-footer in junior high, let it be known that anyone who wanted to pick on Tucker had to go through him first. But unfortunately Joe couldn't be everywhere.

Dora Martinez said she became very concerned when her son Filiberto told her that other students were imitating Tucker's walk and waiting after school to beat him up.

"I couldn't believe kids could be so cruel," she said. "The kids in the neighborhood never did that. He was really being given a hard time."

Paige, now twenty-six, has a real sense of what her brother was going through. Her adolescence, she remembers, was a time when everyone knew who she was simply because of her handicap, because of the way she walked. Never could she be nameless or faceless. Never could she hide out in a crowd. She was Paige-the-handicapped-girl, and that bothered her. So did the questions. Not that they were always cruel. They weren't.

She says she had many good friends who helped her through her teenage years, kind girlfriends who brought her out of herself, helped get her over her shyness. But there always seemed to be questions about how she was feeling because of her walk. It got on her nerves. "You don't necessarily think of having a handicap every day," she says, "but you always do whenever you take a close look at yourself in a full-length mirror. And kids do that a lot as teenagers. Then you realize just how different you are."

Back when Paige was in high school, she wanted desperatedly to go to some of the big dances. But nobody wanted to go out with a girl with cerebral palsy. Then in her senior year at Sharpstown High, a boy did ask her to the prom. She was ecstatic, hardly able to contain her excitement. She got a new dress and had a friend help her with her hair and makeup. She waited and waited for her date to show up, but he never came. She called his home, but there was no answer. She worried that he might have been in an accident. When she saw him at school, she asked him what happened. "You didn't think I really would go to a big dance with someone like you, did you?" the boy said. "That was just a joke."

Still Paige feels sure that adolescence was harder on Tucker than her. He finally came to the realization at that point, she says, that he couldn't go into construction or do heavy work or go into the service. He couldn't do the outdoor things that he had always envisioned doing. How was he going to have a family like his dad had, and be the breadwinner if there was no work he could do?

Paige saw Tucker as terribly confused during that period of his life.

Since his grades were plummeting, Tucker couldn't see himself with any future at all, so he started cutting classes to smoke on street corners. Or he'd go off with other students to listen to the heavy metal music of AC/DC or Metallica. At one point, Terry was so frustrated with his twelve-year-old-cigarette-smoking son that he made Tucker eat cigarettes. That didn't make him stop smoking, nor did making him smoke a cigar until he got sick. Of course, it didn't help that Terry was a smoker, too.

As Tucker's attitude nose-dived, so did Judi's. Her back started acting up again. She gobbled pain pills.

Terry's attitude changed, too. Now the traffic jams bothered him. And he began to notice the tent cities springing up under the bridges, a grim reminder that not everybody found a job in Houston.

Even the neighbors noticed that the family's usual upbeat demeanor would disappear for days at a time.

It went from bad to worse.

There was only one educator that Tucker really respected at Jane Long Middle School—Michael Vaughn. He did everything possible to try and turn Tucker around. Told him he was smart. Told him not to throw his life away. Vaughn would suspend Tucker from school for smoking and then say he'd meet Tucker at night under the street light to help him with his math homework. Tucker didn't take him up on it, didn't want to be treated as special.

For two straight years Tucker had to go to summer school. He didn't mind, because Mr. Vaughn was around to talk to. But then Vaughn died of cancer, and Tucker was devastated. He went to Vaughn's funeral by himself. He walked the streets afterward, crying. Tried to figure it out and he couldn't. Of course, he already knew how unfair life can be. But death, that was another story.

Today all he'll say about it is: "It's hard to believe what can happen to good people."

You talk with Tucker's parents about the middle-school period in Tucker's life and you can tell they're still pained by it. Terry especially. He's not a big man, about five feet, nine inches and slender, with a thin mustache, and he doesn't talk much. Judi thinks that keeping his emotions bottled up over the years forced his heart to deteriorate until he had to have a bypass operation two years ago. For Terry to close his eyes and shake his head when he talks about Tucker's early teen years is a big show of emotion. He blames himself for not carefully quizzing educators as to why Tucker had suddenly become a failure in school.

"We should have made sure he got some special kind of attention," he said. "We assumed the people at school knew what they were doing. You just can't assume that. You have to speak up, ask questions."

Nobody in the family, Terry said, really had an inkling of what was causing Tucker's sudden loss of self-esteem.

"We just didn't know what to do," he said. "He wouldn't do his homework. He didn't really seem to care about anything right then."

Except, of course, baseball. Tucker was still his old self on the field, yelling up a storm. And dreaming big dreams. He saw a life for himself just as it was on the baseball field—with no one hassling him; everyone treating him as one of the guys.

He could see himself playing second base like Billy Doran, who was then the second baseman for the Houston Astros. Small in stature and lacking the physical skills of many of the other professionals, Doran made up for his lack of ability with hustle. Doran had grown up in Cincinnati idolizing Pete Rose, and it showed. He'd jump in the stands after a foul ball. He was the player on the ball club you could hear razzing the opposition while you sat in the stands. No wonder he was Tucker's hero!

Gary McConn, the son of former Houston mayor Jim McConn, and other Sharpstown Little League officials saw to it that, when Tucker was thirteen and fourteen, he played with kids his own size and skill level rather than his own age.

They just couldn't keep the kid who loved baseball more than anybody in the league off the field. They wouldn't be able to live with themselves.

It's hard to imagine what those junior-high years were like for Tucker. Caught in the awkward stage between boy and man or girl and woman, we're all ultra sensitive then anyway. For many of us, though, acne was the worst part. Sure, we were shy and trying to cope with a sudden awareness of the opposite sex, but we were all in the same boat together. We laughed about it with our buddies. But here was a teenager with all the same feelings as other teenagers—he wanted to be seen as a man, attractive to girls, with a good head on his shoulders—coping with a disability that people mocked, that slowed him down in the classroom.

Who could handle that well? Teenage suicides occur over far less.

Tucker would stand around Joe Lyons and other guys who were talking to girls, but never talked to them himself. He was afraid the girls saw him as some kind of weirdo, and nobody wanted to go out with a weirdo. When he walked in a room, he sensed that people started acting differently. Not everybody, but some. The feeling was kind of like what you experience when you walk in on a conversation you're not supposed to hear. When he left a room, he was sure that everything changed behind him, that the other students no longer felt awkward.

Tired of having holes in the toes of his shoes every couple weeks, he started wearing combat boots to school, since they had steel toes and didn't wear out easily. Paige's husband got them for Tucker at a military base. He even thought of joining the Army one day, but he quickly realized that was a dream that didn't have a chance of coming true. The heavy boots, coupled with his semi-squat stance and uneven gait drained his energy a bit more, but it was worth it. He was convinced the holes in the toes of his shoes only drew attention to his walk. Nobody, he was sure, would look at his feet much anymore.

On more than one occasion Tucker thanked God for Little League baseball. There were no problems there. Only fun. He wondered what he'd do without the game the following year. He had made up his mind that he wouldn't play with much younger kids then. He didn't have anything against them, and he wasn't any better than them, that's for sure. He just knew that he wouldn't be able to play with ten-, eleven-, and twelve-year-olds when he was sixteen. He just wouldn't feel right. He was getting close to becoming a man, even if he didn't look it. And barring a miracle, he wouldn't be able to play with boys his own age. He tried not to think too much about how he would feel without baseball. He just wanted to enjoy it now as much as he could. He loved the yelling, having his mother and dad and sisters in the stands rooting for him. Standing at the plate having his family yelling, "Come on, Tucker, you can do it" was like no other feeling in the world. He loved getting dirty from sliding in at second base or home plate. A lot of times he'd slide just to slide. It made him feel as if he was really part of the game. Once he slid in, tore a big hole in his pants in the knee and started bleeding. Everybody asked him how he was. He was safe, that's how he was. He didn't even feel the cut. He had scored a run. Why would he care if he was cut? How many runs did he get to score? Man, he was part of the team!

When some Little League officials said the fifteen-year-old Tucker couldn't play any more, his parents were frightened about what it might do to him. They thought the game was the only thing holding him together. They never would have guessed that the adversity he was about to encounter would be the best thing that could have happened to him.

Instead of breaking him, it made him.

Chapter 5

What surprised many when Tucker was thrust into the national media spotlight was his sense of humor. He's the kind of teenager who'll ask, "Why did the University of Texas scientist stay up every night?" and then laugh harder than the stumped guest as he answers his own question. "He was trying to find a cure for insomnia." He also enjoys the good-natured feud between Texas and Oklahoma. "Did you hear about the Texas redneck who moved to Oklahoma and raised the IQ level of both states?"

Even though he's a transplanted Yankee himself, he loves to dish out the barbs to the people who come from back East. One of his favorites involves a tourist visiting San Antonio.

"What is that building over there?" the tourist asked.

"That, suh," the Texan said, "is the Alamo. That's where 136 Texans held off Santa Anna's fifteen-thousand–man army for four days."

"And that statue of the man on horseback, who's that?" asked the tourist.

"That, suh, is the statue of a Texas Ranger who killed forty-six Apaches in single combat and broke up twenty-seven riots in his lifetime. Say, stranger, where you from anyway?"

"I'm from Boston. You know, we have our heroes there, too. Paul Revere, for instance... "

"Paul Revere?" interrupted the Texan. "You mean that fella who had to ride for help?"

Years after meeting Tucker, people are still surprised by the fact that he told them amusing stories. "He may have cerebral palsy, but he sure is funny," one man told me.

Because most Americans seldom get to know people with disabilities, they expect them to be always in the throes of despair, upset because they're in a wheelchair or not like "normal" people. That kind of expectation, psychologists say, quite naturally makes people reluctant to associate with them. Ignorance definitely isn't bliss. When people envision themselves with some impairment, they can't imagine handling it, let alone laughing and enjoying life. So they're afraid of the disabled people, of what they stand for. Of course, often it does take more guts and more work for a Tucker Church to stay upbeat (often because of the majority's bigotry), but the fact is that he—and many, many other disabled folks—enjoys life. And the disabled can accomplish just as much as anyone else if they aren't held down. History shows that fame and fortune haven't eluded them, but far too many in American society remain amazed they can accomplish much at all, let alone with a smile.

Not long ago at Texas Southern University, a student was genuinely surprised when he learned that Homer and Milton had been blind. "It's hard to believe," he said, "that they could write like that and not be able to see."

Too many of us are still unable to see that a handicap need not deny accomplishment, that it need not be crippling, that it need not rip the joy out of life.

Wheelchair-bound Franklin Roosevelt didn't become a four-term president as a sourpuss. The man exuded a zest for life that left others wishing they could be like him.

Although they were hunchbacks, Poe and Plato have carried many of us to places we never dreamed we could go with their insights. Handel was lame but it didn't stop him from making music that makes your spirit soar. Edison couldn't hear, but he helped us see in the dark.

No one will ever accuse Tucker Church of not trying to escape the cocoon. His parents had a lot to do with that. Again and again you hear people say of Tucker's parents: "They treat him just as if he's normal. (He is, of course, but he walks differently.) They don't let him get away with anything, and they let him do whatever he wants."

Most of the time it is meant as a compliment.

There's no question that attitudes about the disabled have evolved for the better since the late seventies. Otherwise, the Americans With Disabilities Act, which is supposed to guarantee equal treatment and access for those with disabilities, could not have been passed in 1990. But we've still got a long way to go in our attitudes before true equal opportunity for all becomes a reality. We've got to realize that America can't afford to waste any of its potential. Who knows if that child down the street—the one with cerebral palsy—isn't going to be the woman who finally comes up with a cure for cancer ? Or maybe a good butcher or baker or candlestick maker? A good taxpayer.

But the ADA must be implemented equitably! How many new curb cuts have you seen made to enable wheelchairs to roll freely from one side of the street to another? How many handicapped parking spaces have actually been made wide enough for vans with lifts on the sides for wheelchairs? How many businesses still aren't fully accessible? How many proprietors of restaurants still insist—contrary to the law—that a Seeing Eye dog cannot accompany its blind owner inside? How many city or regional bus tours—the basic travel mode for many Americans—have become fully accessible to the disabled? Change is slow.

It could easily be speeded up if schools, Boy Scout troops, social organizations, politicos, and parents tell the truth—that disabled persons are part of a minority that respects no race, sex, age, or class privileges. How many teachers, scoutmasters, coaches, parents, and media outlets remind people that anyone can become disabled from a swimming accident, a traffic mishap, or a slip on the ice? Once we come to fully understand that the only thing that separates us from a wheelchair is a split-second, grinding collision on Main Street, then a nation built for "normal" people over the last two hundred years will truly come to realize that both the physical and mental obstacles created for the disabled must come NOW.

Alfie Kohn, author of the book *The Brighter Side of Human Nature: Altruism and Empathy in Everyday Life*, recently called on schools to care more about producing caring kids. That, of course, makes sense. Tucker Church and black and Hispanic and Asian kids—anybody who's different from the "norm"—might not end up with such a tough go of it if kids were more caring. Would Tucker have been tripped and mocked and called "crip" if students had been shown from day one to be caring and empathetic?

Some will argue that this kind of teaching should be done in the home, but let's face it: it isn't done in a lot of homes. Others will argue that teaching values has no place in schools. As Kohn suggests, whether we like it or not, a teacher imposes his or her values every day on children through methods of discipline, choice of text, tone of voice, presence, and behavior.

Why not include those with disabilities as part of speaking programs at the schools? Why not visit where they work? Once children see that the disabled can function as part of the mainstream, that they laugh and hurt just like the rest of us, apprehension and distrust and anxiety—which often spawn teasing and ridicule—will fall away.

Mary Faithful, an administrator with Houston's Advocacy Inc., an organization dedicated to championing the rights of people with disabilities, points to a 1987 Syracuse University study called "Purposeful Integration... Inherently Equal" for guidance in dealing with the issue of teasing and ridicule of disabled youngsters in the schools. As the study notes, all of us go through some degree of teasing as a child. It's part of growing up. Of course, you don't let it happen if you can avoid it. The study found that in American school programs where disabled children have been integrated most successfully, educators came up with strategies for fostering positive attitudes. They didn't just sit back—as Tucker's schools unfortunately have—and hope positive attitudes would develop on their own. The key to any good program, no matter what the field, is planning and preparation. Had that been done by educators who've dealt with Tucker, chances are his experiences would have been much more positive. He would not have ended up cutting classes because he grew tired of the teasing and ridicule. At Alvin High School, where he is currently a student, Tucker has occasionally been placed in what is known as the "hole" for skipping classes—behavior that took place after he was called "crip" by other students, or deliberately tripped by another student in front of hundreds of students. (The "hole" amounts to an all-day study hall where students judged to be disciplinary problems are sent for days or weeks at a time. No talking or associating with "regular students" is allowed.) Jean Smith, an assistant principal at Alvin High School, explains that Tucker ended up in the "hole" because "he made some bad choices." That is true enough. He shouldn't have skipped school and driven to Galveston. He needed to study government, English, math. He had loved drafting, but he even lost interest in that for a while. Yet educators never tried to find out why things changed.

"None of the administrators ever cared to find out what was happening to him," said Christy Byrne, a school friend of Tucker's. "They just put him in the hole. The more I think about it, the more I think Tucker has wanted to be put in the hole so he didn't have to worry about students calling him names. The school administrators should have looked at the whole picture and worked to make kids have feelings for others."

Today, you frequently hear Judi and Terry Church say that they wish they had been more assertive in dealing with educators. They had always assumed, Judi says, that school officials knew what was best. That is not an uncommon feeling, according to Barbara Cutler, who wrote the book, *Unraveling the Special Education Maze*. She explains:

"Most parents stand in awe of school people and systems because schools represent our childhood images of authority and mystifying expertise. We are all products of school systems and we still retain a number of childlike school behaviors based on old rules."

You have to become more involved, Judi says. Never assume that educators know what's best for your child. Author Cutler says: "Don't be afraid to tell school people what you want for your child. Develop a list of things you want and explain the reasons why you want them."

It is wrong to think that most children are cruel to disabled youngsters. Most aren't. Most are very accepting. Tucker, for example, has developed a strong core of friends and acquaintances. Many are willing to stand up for him at a moment's notice. And yet there are still too many who will give those who are different a hard time. That's why it's critical that school systems develop strategies that show youngsters that we're all in this thing called life together—that everyone benefits when we get along and appreciate each other. Examples are "peer tutoring" and "special friends" programs found in many schools today, where disabled students are paired with mainstream students to help facilitate the whole educational process for the disabled child.

These kinds of learning experiences would also mean no one would be surprised that a kid with cerebral palsy could have a great sense of humor. However, until the day comes when those with disabilities are completely accepted into the community, they must continue to strengthen themselves emotionally for what will come.

Tucker has gotten advice from Ralph Baldwin, the assistant sports editor of *The Houston Post* , who befriended Tucker after learning of his difficulty with Little League. Born with a condition that didn't allow his joints to form properly, Baldwin's right leg is stiff and bends in at the knee. The leg has to be swung around in order for Baldwin to walk. While he has finger movement, Baldwin's wrists are frozen in place and he has no movement in his elbows. He has told Tucker that there will always be people who feel compelled "to act like morons" in the presence of the disabled. "There are some people with a certain maturity level who feel a kind of anxiety in our presence and they act out," Baldwin says.

He was in his forties and on his honeymoon in San Antonio a few years ago when a man began to mock his walk. "My wife and I were walking down the Riverwalk and here was this full-grown man mocking me," Baldwin told Tucker recently. "It's a never-ending deal. Anybody who says it doesn't bother them is lying. But you have to remember they have a problem, not you. All you do is walk differently. You still get where you're going. You can't let them define your life."

The graying, forty-seven-year-old Baldwin, who's five foot four and 125 pounds, has walked all the way down a ramp to get into the Astrodome only to have a security guard walk up to him and ask if he needed a wheelchair. He's gracious now in declining the offer, but he wouldn't have been a few years ago. "You wonder where some people check their brains," he says. "Do they think a helicopter flew down the ramp and dropped me off or what?"

Maturation, Baldwin says, has made him more gracious in dealing with the perpetually immature. Before, he would have come back with an acidic and profane response, much as he did as a boy when a laughing redneck yelled at him from across the parking lot, "Hey, boy, you got that there polio?" Now an active churchgoer, Baldwin doesn't want what he said in response published. It is both funny and profane. "You can't go around all your life with a chip on your shoulder," he now says.

In talking with Tucker, Baldwin has stressed that he can't let "morons" or the "immature" make him feel bad about himself. He wants Tucker to understand that he can be in charge of his life. That kind of talk from a man who's undergone the same kind of stress has seemed to work on Tucker. "Mr. Baldwin's really neat," Tucker said. "He's just kept bouncing back from things the way I have to."

Baldwin acknowledges that one of the toughest things a disabled boy has to deal with is dating. You never know, he says, if a girl won't go out with you because of the way you look. "It's always in the back of your mind and something you just have to deal with," he says. "It's not easy."

Tucker realizes that in some ways Baldwin had it even tougher than him. "At least I could play Little League and ride a bike, and he never could," Tucker says.

Even though he knew he couldn't ride a two-wheeler, Baldwin remembers staying up one Christmas Eve praying he'd get one. "I wanted to ride a bike more than anything, but I just never could because of my leg."

Baldwin says he really didn't get a heavy volume of taunts as a youth, but when he got them they always hurt. "It made you wish you could get the handicap lifted from you somehow," he says. "It is a heavy burden, but I never felt defeated by it. Now I just consider my handicap a minor annoyance."

Growing up in Little Rock, Arkansas, Baldwin said he was fortunate to have parents who let him stand on his own. They wanted him to try as much as he could. He did see, however, other disabled youths who were so protected by family and friends that they were permanently disabled. "There was just no way they could ever compete in the outside world with that kind of background."

Baldwin believes that business managers are generally skeptical about employing the disabled. He senses that they're unsure whether someone who looks so different can do the job. In the back of his mind, he always wonders whether he's gotten passed over for a job because of how he looks. "It's something you can never know, but you can't let it eat you up."

On a recent trip out to Tucker's home in Alvin, Baldwin let him know that he thought attitudes toward the disabled have improved a lot since he was a boy. People, he said, seem more willing to give the disabled a chance now.

That was certainly the case in Tucker's Little League experience. Everybody connected with his local Sharpstown Little League, save one, wanted him to enjoy his time in the league. Only the Little League hierarchy, which is controlled from Williamsport, Pennsylvania, were, and are, way out in left field. They do what they can to handicap the handicapped. They believe in segregation. Even though Tucker Church in Houston, Larry Anderson in Arizona, and Julie Henry in Pennsylvania could function just fine on a Little League playing field, the Little League brass preferred them in a special Challenger league, away from "normal kids."

"I really think that I don't live up to what their standard of perfection is for kids on the ball field," said thirteen-year-old Julie Henry, who can hear only in one ear. "It just doesn't make any sense that I can do everything else with regular kids but because I've got a special hearing aid they don't want me in Little League. In some ways, I feel sorry for the people who run Little League. They're sick and don't know it."

The more mainstreaming of the disabled that is done, the better it is for everyone. For Tucker, playing regular Little League baseball gave him the sense that he could participate on the playing field of life. To all his teammates, it was a wonderful learning experience, making them realize that a different way of walking and throwing did not mean an individual was crazy.

"I thought if somebody was handicapped and walked weird he had to really be dumb or be weird upstairs, but Tucker was just like us except he couldn't run right," observed thirteen-year-old Mark Sartain, a former teammate of Tucker's. "He just wanted to have fun. Playing with him changed my opinion of the handicapped."

Tom Churpek, another former teammate of Tucker's, echoed Mark and went even further.

"It pretty much changed the whole way I thought about people," the thirteen-year-old said. "You really do have to judge people on what they have inside. If you don't, you're going to make some terrible mistakes about people and that's not fair."

Wonderful insights from youngsters so young. Make no mistake about it: they'll pass on what they've learned to others. That's how things will change for the better for America's disabled.

The same valuable lessons were learned by those who played with Julie Henry in the Guilford, Pennsylvania, Little League and those who experienced the coaching of the wheelchair-bound Lawrence Anderson in Phoenix, Arizona. You would think that any organization that could afford that kind of learning experience to children would be excited to do so. Unfortunately, legal battles have become necessary for them to remain with their Little League teams.

Chapter 6

Even when he was featured as an inspirational speaker before five thousand people during the insurance industry's 1992 Million Dollar Round Table meeting, Tucker used his wit to wow the Chicago gathering. Wearing a suit and tennis shoes in the David Letterman tradition, a smiling Tucker walked in his herky-jerky fashion up to the podium with his mother, and shared the Sylvester the Cat anecdote from his elementary school days—"I couldn't figure out how they knew it was me in the costume"—and played it for a laugh.

So goes the mystery and beauty of life. The teenager who's only alive because of a miracle, who's suffered tremendous physical and emotional pain because of cerebral palsy, is the one everyone can count on to make them feel better.

Later, Tucker sat in a coffee shop with some of the insurance men and shared one of his favorite stories:

> An elderly Houston woman died and appeared at the Pearly Gates. When Saint Peter asked for her credentials, she proudly presented her Houston Symphony membership, receipts from Neiman-Marcus and the Ritz Carlton Hotel, and a picture of herself shaking hands with the editor of *The Houston Post*. Saint Peter, deeply impressed, said, "Come in, Madam, but I don't think you'll like it."

The response to his joke was so good Tucker served up another:

Two tough Oklahoma truckers stopped at a small diner outside Houston. It didn't take them long to get in an argument with some Texas ranchers. "You guys want to tear each other apart," shouted the waitress, "go on outside."

The Okie truckers walked out the door with the Texas ranchers right behind them. Within five minutes, the Texans were back.

"What happened?" asked the waitress.

"Them dogs from Oklahoma pulled out razors."

"My God! No kidding!"

"It turned out okay. They didn't have a place to plug 'em in."

Humor seems to erase Tucker's pain, but Tucker says he stores and catalogues jokes because he wants to use them one day in his work as a disc jockey; he likes to make people laugh. When you grin after he tells you that Texas occupies all of the continent of North America except the small part set aside for the United States, Mexico, and Canada, it makes him feel good. If you groan after he suggests that Oklahomans don't eat dill pickles because they can't get their heads in the jar, he's on an upper.

The more you're around him, the more you realize just how much he dislikes dwelling on the downers in his life. He wants to look forward, not backward.

Tucker talks about the struggles in his life only because he hopes that by doing so he can change the way people deal with the disabled. Maybe, he says, his story will give others an easier time of it.

He wants to see every child get a fair chance at using all of his or her talents. He knows that not every child who's disabled can effectually shrug off ridicule. Come to think of it, he says, he still hasn't shrugged it all off. There's still a bit of a chip on his shoulder and still pain he has to work through.

How do you forget jerks walking up behind you and imitating your walk and laughing? He saw how ridicule paralyzed his sister Paige for years. What if Paige hadn't met a wonderful man? Would she have blossomed, or could she have ended up house bound, with TV replacing Barbie dolls?

How many other children, he wonders, are imprisoned by the hopelessness that grows inside them like a weed when people suggest they can't do this and can't do that?

What if you're not lucky enough to have the Parsells living down the street, people who show by example that a handicap need not be crippling?

Tucker knows that not every disabled child has parents who have the courage to allow their child to become as independent as he can be. He's well aware that his parents caught some criticism for allowing him to ride a bike and skateboard, and engage in practically every athletic endeavor he wanted to do.

Whenever he received stitches—and he may have gotten more than a hundred from falls during childhood accidents—some would doubt the wisdom of his parents' letting him try to do what other children did. They thought he should be pampered, pitied, pushed to the side. Just as Little League did.

"People have to realize that you have to do as much as you can so you can be strong," Tucker says. "If my experiences can make a difference for some people, that would be great."

Chapter 7

Parents of Little Leaguers are notorious for calling newspapers, TV stations—even the cops occasionally—in an attempt to get their child more playing time. Their little Johnny, they'll tell you, wouldn't be riding the bench if he was given an equal opportunity to show his stuff. If the coach wouldn't discriminate against a kid with long hair, short hair, curly hair, red hair, crooked teeth, or a pimply nose, then Johnny could be the next Roger Clemens. One lady who sounded sane even called me at *The Houston Post* to see if I thought the Equal Employment Opportunity Commission would investigate her son's lack of action at second base.

When you write a local newspaper column dedicated to righting wrongs, you hear from a lot of angry parents of Little Leaguers. Angry Little League managers and coaches call, too. They'll claim an ump's on the take, accepting free love from one boy's mother and free goldfish from another. Not the kind of claims that are easy to substantiate. You dismiss them as coming from pathetic but harmless types who try to find through their children an athletic glory (and maybe big money) that they never had. Unfortunately, not all their anger can be vented through phone calls to the media. You see them shaking or cuffing or screaming at ten-year-old children who don't perform the way the parents would like. Sometimes one parent beats another. In 1984, Houston Little League coach Cameron Dobos died after he was punched out by another coach.

But it didn't take me long to realize that Judi Church's complaint about Little League was unlike any I had heard. She was sobbing as she talked about her son, about the hard time he had been having lately. My only reservation about what she told me was that she must be leaving something out. I didn't think Little League officials could be so cold. I was wrong. At both the local and national level, they couldn't have cared less about Tucker.

That's the way it goes, the Little League honchos said. Tough luck. Tucker couldn't play. He was too old.

Earlier that year, Tucker had signed up to play for a senior team in the Sharpstown Little League in Houston, Texas, but both his mother and a coach, Scott Davis, soon realized the fifteen-year-old's limited physical abilities would never enable him to make a team in the thirteen- to fifteen-year-old age bracket.

"But I just couldn't see this kid not play baseball," Davis said. "He loved it so much."

During his previous eight years in Little League, Tucker had never even managed to bat .200, but he did lead the league in yelling "Fire it in there!" to the pitcher from center field. And when one of his teammates came to the plate, Tucker was the one who always yelled, "You can do it!"

When Davis asked Tucker if he'd mind playing for the Pirates, a team of nine- to twelve-year-olds, kids his size, he wasn't happy. It was the year he had hoped he could play with the big guys, the year his game would come together and he could show his stuff. In his last year of Little League, he wanted to play in the big time. For the last two years he had been playing with younger kids because his mother and coaches thought it safer. But he had grown a quarter-inch and put on a pound in the last year. Why wasn't that enough? Also he seldom fell down running to first base anymore.

Davis told Tucker that his coordination hadn't improved enough for him to play safely with boys his own age. He couldn't hit the faster pitching nor could he catch the harder hitting. Other Little League coaches agreed. But Davis said that when he told Little League District Administrator Paul Goolsby and his aide Gus Benis before the season that the Sharpstown league was hoping to waive the age rule for the youngster with cerebral palsy, Goolsby warned him that he had never heard of national Little League officials okaying such an arrangement. Goolsby partially corroborates that story, saying he remembers that Davis wanted to waive the age rule for an older child. Goolsby said, however, he was never told that Tucker had cerebral palsy.

"He's lying because he knows he looks bad," Davis said. "I never would have tried to get him to waive the age rule without a heavy extenuating circumstance. And nobody else in Sharpstown would have either."

The Sharpstown Little League board, which had approved the arrangement for Tucker in the previous two years, gave the go-ahead. It was safer and it would make a kid who loved baseball happy. At first, Tucker was reluctant to play for the Pirates. It was a blow to his ego to play with the younger kids again. But it didn't take long for his old spark to return. At least he was doing what he loved, playing baseball. He figured he had to still be playing on a team if his dreams were ever going to come true.

A project manager for a fire alarm company, Davis started coaching in Little League in 1982, two years before his son Sean was born. His wife Sandi always seems nearby. They're one of those couples who feel it's their duty to help in the community. The Davises displayed genuine affection in public. It's not often you see a coach holding his wife's hand behind the backstop, but the Davises were often that way.

They'd stand there and talk about how their sons would do one day in Little League. "It'll be so cute," Sandi would say and Scott would nod. She's the talker in the family, not him. Even when the Tucker Church episode exploded, she'd explain what happened and he'd nod until he heard something he didn't agree with. "Now Sandi, that's not quite right," he'd say and then explain the situation as he knew it. He abhorred the publicity the ban had brought, even trying to change a game's starting time so the media wouldn't be there. "I don't want these kids, particularly Tucker, treated like some kind of freaks," he said. "They're just good kids who got caught up in some adult ugliness."

The Davises had been moved by newspaper stories that pointed out the rising number of young boys in trouble with the law. Organized competition, they felt, would give kids a good way to spend their time and perhaps a positive foundation to build on. Scott would be there coaching and Sandi would be watching, learning how to keep the official score book so she'd be ready to help out when her sons played.

Tucker was eleven when Scott first met him. He watched him play and was immediately struck by his zest for life. He'd hit the ball to third base, and if he fell down on the way to first, he'd get back up and run harder than ever. "I'd never seen such gumption in my life," Davis said. Four years later, when he saw a chance for the youngster to continue competing, he moved on it. "We knew it was a technical violation of the age rule, but it seemed like there should have been some way to waive it. As it turned out, there was. Little League, though, just doesn't like to deal with the hassle. The men who run it at the top get so much into the power thing that they forget that they're supposed to be helping kids."

It appeared Davis's Pirates might finish second, which meant they'd make the playoffs. Tucker hit only .167 for the year, but he did lead the league in reminding teammates that a game isn't over until the fat lady sings.

It had been an uneventful season until Bob Whitfill, the manager of the Brewers, realized his club might not beat the Pirates for the playoffs. He didn't like the fact his team might not get the big trophies. No longer did he think it was okay for the Pirates to play a fifteen-year-old boy on a team of nine- to twelve-year-olds.

"Somebody has to abide by the rules," said Whitfill, who saw to it that the Little League district administrator, Paul Goolsby, heard about Tucker. It took Goolsby, by his own estimation, about ten seconds to figure out what to do. If it was true, Tucker couldn't play and Davis couldn't coach.

He sent an aide, Gus Benis, to talk to Sharpstown Little League officials to see if it was true that an over-age boy was playing. Benis said he found out through Sharpstown Little League President Lercy Simoneaux and Coach Scott Davis that it was. Benis said he was never told, nor did he ask, why an older boy was playing in a younger bracket—a claim hotly disputed by Simoneaux and Davis.

"I told Goolsby and Benis even before the season that Tucker had cerebral palsy and I told him again," Davis said. "He's making it sound like we tried to smuggle a fifteen-year-old onto a team of twelve-year-olds for no reason. That's insane. The whole league knew. We knew the age rule. The whole point was trying to make an exception for a kid with a handicap."

Simoneaux was incredulous when he heard that Benis claimed not to know that Tucker didn't have cerebral palsy.

"Of course Benis knew," Simoneaux said. "Do you think we wouldn't tell him that? My God, that's why we made the decision! We'd never play an over-age boy unless there was an over-riding reason. Our whole Sharpstown board was in on the decision. There was nothing hidden. The fact was that Goolsby and Benis believed rules are rules are rules no matter what. Later they realized how awful it looked that they went after a disabled kid, so they tried to change their stories. These power-hungry guys just make you sick. They ruin Little League."

Simoneaux and Davis said Benis told them that if Tucker played and Davis coached, the Sharpstown league could lose its charter—in other words, no longer be part of Little League. In sworn testimony later, Benis said he didn't tell Simoneaux to ask Davis to resign.

He was trying to split hairs.

"I didn't say resign," Benis said. "The statement was I felt like he should turn him loose."

Sandi Davis said she talked to Goolsby to find out what was happening and he was so angry that he told her that their son Sean wouldn't be able to play Little League in Sharpstown as long as he was in charge.

Sandi Davis said she'll never forget Goolsby's parting words to her. "You can't ever break rules. I don't care who's involved."

Simoneaux, then thirty-three with three boys in Little League, was stunned by Goolsby's anger. And he became incensed when he later learned that Little League had an age-waiver rule that it doesn't inform even league presidents about.

"I had let Tucker on a team because it was the right thing to do. That's what America is supposed to be about, doing the right thing. What happened there left such a bad taste in my mouth that I took my kids out of Little League. We ended up canceling all the playoff games because the coaches were just sick of dealing with the organization."

Terry Fry, an attorney who's done litigation on behalf of Little League's insurance companies, believes Little League officials may not readily give out information about the age-waiver rule because they fear a huge onslaught of people trying to get exceptions to the rule.

If Goolsby didn't know about the age-waiver rule after thirty years as district administrator, it was the only rule he didn't know. He's the kind of guy who says, "I know every rule in Little League backwards and forwards," repeatedly and without prompting. But then he also says he didn't know anything about an age-waiver rule. "No, I really didn't know," he says. Sometimes he seems to contradict himself. "I don't know why they didn't try to get a waiver before the season," he says. "They have to know they could have gotten one."

Does that mean Goolsby knew about the age-waiver rule?

"Oh, no, I didn't know anything about it," he says.

Confusing statements, to say the least.

Davis called Tucker to tell him he could no longer

play. The boy's crying made the coach break down in tears. For the first time before a game, Tucker didn't dream. He lay awake, wondering what it all meant. All he could figure out is that lately he had seemed to be meeting an awful lot of mean people. He wondered if it was something he was doing that made them that way.

Not long after Judi Church called me, I called National Little League headquarters in Williamsport, Pennsylvania. The reaction of a top official, Elmer Lehotsky, was strange. After listening to what was happening to Tucker in Houston—that a furor had begun among the citizenry— he admitted there was a special waiver program allowing children to play in a particular age group if a doctor thought it best: "For the children who by a quirk of nature are limited, we've been giving them special consideration." But then he conceded that no local Little League officials or parents had been informed of the waiver program. He also said the program had never been put in writing. I asked him if legal liability was the reason. No, he said. Was it because National Little League officials didn't want to be bothered with ruling on waivers from around the country? Clearly nervous, he tried to explain. "We forgot to put the information out," he said.

Year after year after year they forgot to put the information out?

In 1993 I asked Lehotsky if it were possible that Goolsby, who had been a district administrator for more than thirty years, couldn't have known about the age waiver. "It's possible," he said. "He may have missed a meeting where it was talked about."

Would Little League have only had one meeting in thirty years where the age waiver is talked about?

"I don't know," Lehotsky said.

Anything's possible, of course. But it seems more likely that Little League, which has set up special leagues for the disabled in an effort to segregate them, was doing

everything it could to discourage Tucker from playing in
a regular league. Documents in other discrimination cases
filed by the disabled suggest that National Little League
officials would rather not bother with the disabled.

Still, Lehotsky said, even though Tucker's parents and
his manager and Tucker's Little League president knew
nothing about an age waiver, they should have had sense
enough to ask national headquarters in Williamsport about
an age waiver before the season. If that's not confusing,
nothing is.

"If the mother can get a doctor to say he should play
in that age group, her son may be able to play again this
year," Lehotsky said. "Our charter committee here will
vote on it."

It was Thursday, May 25, 1989, when Lehotsky and I
talked. I told him that Tucker's last game might well be
the following day. If his team lost, there would be no
playoff action. The boy understood, I said, that unless his
body went through the miraculous transformation he so
often dreamed about, this would be his last year of
organized ball. Tucker realized he wasn't good enough to
play at a higher level of amateur baseball. I also told
Lehotsky what Tucker had told me: "I can handle not
playing again if I know when I'm playing my last game. I
can get psyched for it, you know what I mean? But ending
baseball like this kills me. Nothing's been going right for
me but baseball."

If a doctor faxed information to Williamsport, I asked,
could Lehotsky's committee take action so Tucker could
play in what may be his last game of organized baseball?

"Oh, no," Lehotsky replied, surprised that such a
question would be asked. "We would never get a quorum
Friday. Everybody's on holiday (for Memorial Day). The
boy will just have to wait."

Talk about insensitivity!

I wrote a piece on Tucker's situation that appeared on
the front page of *The Houston Post* on the morning the

Pirates were to play their last regular season game. Though I didn't realize it at the time, something Tucker had said during our interview indicated that this experience was going to make him, not break him.

"I don't think they should have done this to Scott," Tucker said. "He's a good coach for kids. Sure I want to play, but here's a guy who tried to help kids not able to coach anymore. It's not right. Even if they say I can play, I won't, unless Scott can coach."

The story, which was picked by the Associated Press and wired to news organizations across the country, touched off an avalanche of criticism of Little League officials. Television crews made their way to Tucker's home. Disc jockeys asked Tucker to come on their shows. Radio talk shows throughout the United States used the story to argue that Little League had forgotten its mission of helping children enjoy playing America's pastime.

"The phones went wild when we talked about it on the air," said Tony Angelo, producer of Glenn Beck's morning show on Houston 104 FM.

Five petitions drawn up by one hundred parents and coaches of the Sharpstown Little League were fired off to national, state, and local Little League officials. Their message was clear:

"...If certain rules cannot be waived for a courageous boy and a compassionate coach, then we have made this game much too serious and have sadly passed an opportunity to show our children what this league should be all about, and what, in the final analysis, is really important...

"...Coach Davis exemplifies sportsmanship in the true spirit of Little League Baseball, and his actions should be applauded, not censured. If objections to his roster were to be raised, they should have been put forward at the beginning of the season, not during the last week race for playoff position...

"We, the undersigned coaches and parents of the Sharpstown Little League Minors, respectfully request that Scott Davis be reinstated immediately as manager of the minor league Pirates, and that all his other positions and duties within the league be restored without qualification..."

Little League officials in Williamsport soon got an earful of the outrage. Astounded by the hundreds of angry phone calls made to their headquarters from across the country, they suddenly ruled that Tucker could play in the game scheduled that night if he presented a doctor's note at game time that said he'd be safer playing on a team of younger boys.

Miraculously, they got the quorum together that Lehotsky had said was impossible. Not for the boy's sake, but for public relations' sake.

Dr. James "Red" Duke, a physician well acquainted with Tucker's condition and a doctor well-known to Texans because of his weekly TV appearances on health issues, was eloquent in his letter to Little League district administrator Paul Goolsby. The note from the professor at the University of Texas Health Science Center at Houston should hang in the entrance to every Little League office:

Dear Mr. Goolsby:

The institution of Little League Baseball in the United States is a program for young people that has no equal. The volunteers that make this possible will never receive the credit that they are due for the contributions that they make to the vast numbers of youngsters all across the nation. I am very cognizant of the need for regulations, and I am most respectful of the wisdom and principle that cause these issues to be generated. There are times, however, when the overall good would be best served by some amendment of the rules. Such is the case with Tucker Church.

Everyone will agree that the Little League Baseball concept has been created and is conducted for the children. Its incredible success is a direct function of that which it has contributed to the developing lives of the participants. Although we like to think that we are all created equal, we all in honesty have to admit that this utopian condition does not exist. I would not pretend to suggest that I could design better rules for determining a means by which different types of children could qualify to play in any particular league.

In the case of Tucker Church, the young man desires desperately to participate. He has participated, in spite of enormous handicaps. The wisdom of his coach to have him play in a younger age group than that for which he chronologically qualifies is probably a wise one. It has allowed him to play and feel a part of a team, even though he is not physically capable of participating with men of his own age. There is no question that his limitations are of such nature that he does not have strength or coordination to be able to compete safely with young men between the ages of thirteen and fifteen.

It is abundantly clear to all of us that there is some risk in participating in any sport. We should also be cognizant of the fact that there are significant differences in an individual's strength and agility at almost every year of development. Unless there is some other overriding reason other than age group limitations and physical prowess, I think it would be very appropriate to allow him to participate in an activity that means so much to his self-esteem and sense of belonging. He is at greater risk for injury trying to play with the young men of his own age group.

If there is anything more I can do to assist you in this important issue, I trust you will make your needs known to me. I would strongly urge you to give serious consideration to amending the rules to make it possible for him to participate in the activity among a group of young people.

Sincerely,
James H. Duke, Jr., M.D.

Dr. John Harris, the chairman of the department of radiology at Hermann Hospital wrote a shorter letter to Little League officials, but it certainly got its point across:

"...Tucker Church, a child (age fifteen) with cerebral palsy, is small-framed and underweight because of his condition. He cannot compete with boys of his own age, but I know of no medical reason why he cannot play baseball with boys closer to his size."

Even as Tucker's father was asking doctors if they could write letters, the seventy-three-year-old Goolsby called Tucker's mother and warned her not to bother.

"He told me that even if I got the medical statement that league officials required, he'd make sure it would never fly," Judi Church said. "It was so strange. He was threatening me. He said he'd see to it that Tucker wouldn't play. He said we had to live under the rules as he knew them at the time."

Goolsby, who says he tapes many of his phone calls, particularly those dealing with Little League, said he wouldn't characterize his call to Judi Church as threatening, but he wouldn't allow me to listen to the tape of the conversation.

Though he knew full well that Tucker's parents would be scurrying around right up until game time to get the proper medical documentation, Goolsby didn't show up at Bayland Park to read Dr. Duke's letter. He stayed at his home ten miles away and waited for the letter to be brought to him.

"I didn't want to expose myself to those people there," he said.

Besides, he said, it wasn't his job to go to Little League games. He seldom went. His job, he said, is to help people follow the rules. He knew all the rules. Except, of course, for the age-waiver rule. Goolsby never did give his official okay for the game. Nor did Little League headquarters.

In fact, Sharpstown Little League President Lercy Simoneaux said he was warned through one of Goolsby's lieutenants that the league's charter might be withdrawn and that there might not be an all-star game if Davis coached his team's last game.

"I was only doing," Goolsby said, "what was good for Little League. Rules must be followed."

Worried that Goolsby would make good on his threat and remove the league's charter, Davis told Simoneaux he wouldn't coach. "I don't want all the kids to suffer because of me," he said. But that meant Tucker wouldn't play.

"I'm not going to play unless Coach Davis coaches and that's final," Tucker said. "I'm standing up for what's fair."

The little guy with the twisted and bent legs and arms who loved to chatter to his teammates, "When the going gets tough, the tough get going," was doing just that.

As Tucker stood by the ball field, three F-14s streaked overhead. He tried to make light of what was happening. "They're in the missing-man formation," he said. "They must be doing it for me."

After conferring again with Simoneaux, Davis coached. Neither man wanted Tucker to sit out what now looked for sure like his last game of organized baseball. The Pirates were already behind by five runs. A half-hour after the Pirates' game with the A's began, Tucker entered the lineup.

Only twenty-four hours had passed since the brouhaha had developed. No one knew it then—never would have guessed it—but what happened would dramatically change Tucker Church's life for the better. And what happened in that day's time would make the country look at Little League baseball as it never had before. Because when they looked, people didn't like what they saw, and they began to ask questions. (As it turned out, the institution's behavior toward a handicapped boy would be used to fuel legal proceedings in another case that would last seven years—a case that cost Little League more than one million dollars and demonstrated a callousness on the part of the organization that you usually see evidenced only in a sociopath.)

As Tucker came to the plate in the third inning, TV cameras were there to capture the moment. Tucker was now the main man, not the missing man.

The crowd of one hundred people screamed his name. "Tucker, Tucker," they chanted. Five pitches later, he struck out.

"I swung as hard as I could," he said, shaking his head. "I don't know what he threw me. I'm not sure I saw it."

"I'm so proud of him," said Tucker's mother Judi, who sat weeping in the stands.

Tucker had no fielding chances or hits during the game, but once again he led the team in yells of encouragement to the pitcher. After his team lost 13–4, he was carried off the field on the shoulders of players from both teams.

A little later, he broke down in tears. He couldn't stop sobbing as his father led him to the car.

"I did it," he cried. "I did it."

He was happier than he had been in a long time.

You may be surprised why.

"The thing so important to me is that I didn't play until Scott coached. I wanted to play bad. More than just about anything, because I knew I wouldn't be playing on a team again. But how could I play if he didn't coach? That wouldn't be fair. Why should he have to suffer for doing right? He loved coaching kids. He's the one who gave me a chance. All I've ever wanted is to be treated fair and I couldn't turn around and not be, you know what I mean? I felt like I finally stood up for what was right. Of all the good things that happened to me because of my fight with Little League, I still think that was the most important. I found I could stand up for what was right even though it would hurt me."

When people had mocked his walk or made fun of him, he hadn't stood up to them the way he would have liked. He had worried that he'd get beaten to a pulp. He hadn't said anything to teachers when he couldn't write fast enough to keep up, because he thought it would make him look stupid. But he had stood up for Scott, a guy who had treated him fairly. He remembers that when he went to bed that night he had a huge smile on his face. And once again he dreamed.

He saw himself as a disc jockey.

Chapter 8

The phone rang. It was early morning in the Church household, the day after Tucker's big Little League game. If the sun had come up, everyone in the family was too tired to see it. The voice on the other end of the phone wanted to know if Tucker would be the morning guest with Glenn Beck on radio station KRBE 104 FM. Word is that Tucker's excited "Yes" almost shattered the eardrum of the producer on the other end of the phone.

Everything in the days immediately following the confrontation with Little League was like a dream for Judi Church. The response by people on talk shows and in letters to the editor kept her alternating between smiles and tears. She couldn't remember feeling so good in a long time. Her boy was seeing what she had told him, that there were a lot of good people out there. She had been afraid that his junior-high experience was warping him, that it would, in fact, cripple his chance for a productive future. But now he was seeing that many, many people were decent, loving, caring people who wanted to see the right thing done. The glass is half-full, not half-empty. Before her eyes she saw her son reclaiming the spirit he had had as a tyke.

She knew Tucker was so proud of standing up for Scott, of not playing until he coached. It was a stand that made him feel like a man. And then each supportive call to their home, each favorable story on the nightly newscast, each story in the newspaper—together they propelled him

from despair to hope. Her son's spirit soared as it hadn't
since that time years earlier when he had hit that little
grounder and managed to run around all the bases.

When Tucker entered the radio control room, I was
with him. His eyes got THIS BIG. It was the kind of place
he dreamed about, where one day he'd tell his jokes and
entertain millions. He stood up to the microphone. His first
words on live radio? "Hi, everybody, it's a beautiful day."

So it was. He talked about baseball and wanting to
become a disc jockey. He made sure he didn't look at his
mother, whom he could hear weeping in the background.
He knew if he did, he would have started crying, too.
Nobody wants to cry on live radio, especially on their
first gig.

He handled the sudden fame carefully, with a maturity
far beyond his years. He enjoyed shaking everybody's
hand, but he also wondered if some of the people might
be the kind who made fun of people like him. He didn't
want to think that way, but, hey, he knew what he knew.
When he went back to school, he noticed that some
students who had given him a hard time were acting
friendly. He didn't call that to their attention, but he
catalogued their behavior away in his brain. He also vowed
to stay close to those who had been his friends, even if
they weren't the school's elite. They had cared about him
when he was nobody. He suspected that those who hadn't
liked him before only did so now because of all the
attention he'd received.

Little League's treatment of Tucker Church had spawned
a reaction among Americans that ranged from shock to
anger to tears.

Bob Greene, the syndicated Pulitzer-prize-winning
columnist for the *Chicago Tribune*, urged the editors of
Sports Illustrated to give what is perhaps the highest honor
in all of sports—the magazine's designation as Sportsman
of the Year—to both Tucker and his coach, Scott Davis.

"There will be athletic performances this year that
display more agility, strength and power," Greene wrote.
"But as far as a lot of us are concerned, the balloting for

Sportsman of the Year—for Sportsmen of the Year—is already over, and the two winners are glorious almost beyond words."

When Greene's column relating the struggles of Tucker, and his coach was reprinted in *Reader's Digest*, it received the most mail of any article in the magazine's history.

While *The New York Times* ran an article on Tucker under the headline, "Hero Lifts Team Spirit," *San Diego Union* columnist Barry Lorge wrote that the kids and the parents of Sharpstown "deserve a standing ovation for standing up to mindless bureaucracy.

"Little League should not be an exercise in cutthroat competition," Lorge said in his May 31, 1989, column. "It is supposed to be fun for the participants, a learning experience without big league pressure. There is something to be said for teaching respect for rules, of course, but real-life education should show youngsters that there are circumstances where the best rule is to make a sensible exception."

Columnist Rick Casey of the *San Antonio Light* was blunt: "So why did the defeated Pirates carry little Tucker Church off the field on their shoulders?

"Because Tucker had become a symbol of the stupidity and meanness of some hypercompetitive adults. More than that, though, he became the symbol of one victory for big hearts over little minds."

Pundits wondered if this was evidence of yet another American institution falling victim to the power-hungry and selfish. The fact that this institution directly involved children made it particularly worrisome to mothers and fathers across the country.

Had they cared, National Little League officials would have been more than a little concerned by the outpouring of support for Tucker. No one sympathized with the organization's original position. They should have learned that they were going down the wrong path. But they've continued on the same road, unwilling to make accommodations for the disabled even as the nation's leaders have enacted legislation banning discrimination against them.

They were, and are, out of touch.

The stories on the dispute that ran on the network news and in hometown newspapers spawned letter writing to everyone connected with the affair.

Rebecca Haidt of St. Louis, Missouri, sent an angry and perceptive letter to Little League national president Creighton Hale, and she passed on a copy to Tucker and his family.

> "What disappointed me most... was district administrator Paul Goolsby's lack of compassion. But even if compassion were not the issue... what purpose does the Little League, at base, serve, other than fostering in boys and girls a sense of teamwork, a betterment of physical coordination, and a spirit of healthy competition? And what purpose did Scott Davis's coaching of Tucker Church (in no matter which age group) serve other than all of the above? Is Goolsby... supposed to send a message to the children of America that disabled children have no right to develop their understanding of teamwork, competition and also develop their coordination? If this is indeed what we learn from Goolsby's actions, then his actions bring shame and dishonor to the American values at stake in the Little League and what it brings to children.
>
> "...It is equally disgraceful that a good, compassionate coach (a boon to any children's team of any age anywhere) was asked to resign from coaching because of his work with and sympathy for Tucker Church. How disappointing it is that the Little League honors rules and winning more than it does the true spirit of competition and the basic American (and human) values: freedom for all to participate toward their goals, healthy

competition, fitness of mind and body, and just treatment of one person by another. I regret the Little League's handling of this situation and am deeply disappointed in the organization..."

Eileen Foppiano of Boston, Massachusetts, wrote an open letter to Coach Davis in *The Boston Globe*. "You have taught these youngsters compassion for their fellow man," she wrote, "which is a far greater lesson than they could ever learn in Little League."

A veteran cop, San Diego police Detective Steve Casey, felt compelled to write directly to Davis: "Just a note of thanks from a baseball fan... for making sure that Tucker Church gets to play baseball on your team. You and Tucker and all of his past, present and future teammates are a class act, and very special people..."

In her letter to Davis, Mary Huyck of Greenwich, Connecticut, thanked him "for being a voice of reason and decency."

Chicago attorney Frederick Cohn offered free legal help to the Church family in his letter. It was refused. "We don't want any money from Little League," Judi Church said. "We just want them to learn to treat kids decently."

You could sense Mrs. Robbie Kelley's angry tears in the letter she wrote to Little League headquarters from Chelsea, Alabama:

"...I have a twenty-year-old daughter who has had cerebral palsy since she was six months old. She only weighs thirty-six pounds. Do you think I would let somebody do her like Tucker and get away with it? No, I wouldn't. It is time us parents with children like this stand up for their rights and show people they can't be pushed around..."

Little League's Goolsby, remains unapologetic today about his behavior. He now says Tucker should have never been allowed to play Little League ball in the first place. He says that, because Tucker didn't have good balance, he could have fallen as he ran and struck someone with his head, hurting another child. "You have to take safety into account," Goolsby said.

Does it surprise Goolsby that in Tucker's eight years of Little League play, he never ran into people with his head and hurt them?

"You never know when something bad can happen," he said.

Goolsby does admit that he never saw Tucker play. What he had heard from his lieutenants, he said, convinced him that Tucker was a clear and present danger to other youngsters.

Chapter 9

The caller on the other end of the phone line said he was with The Houston Astros baseball team.

"You're kidding," Judi Church said.

"No, I'm not," the caller said. "We want Tucker to throw out the first pitch at Saturday night's Astros–Dodgers game and for your whole family to be our guests."

"You're kidding," Judi Church said.

The caller wasn't kidding. On June 4, 1989, Tucker got to throw out the first pitch at the Astrodome.

It was a beautiful gesture by the Astros. Even the team's by-the-letter millionaire owner, John McMullen, couldn't stomach Little League's behavior. Neither could the team's most win-at-all-costs players.

Astros all-star relief pitcher Dave Smith couldn't have been any more direct. "Where do you go to picket? That's the biggest bleep I've ever heard."

Before the game, Bill Doran, Tucker's hero, brought him an autographed bat. Mike Scott, a Cy Young award-winning pitcher, signed one of his baseballs. Slugger Glenn Davis, who's now with the Baltimore Orioles, added to the autographed bat collection. Hall of Famer Yogi Berra, a Houston coach, signed a ball.

Houston Post sports columnist Kenny Hand, Tucker's favorite sportswriter, interviewed him for a column.

"I couldn't believe what was happening," Tucker said. "I was there a lot of times before but never on the field level or around the players. I'll tell you, the Astrodome really is an engineering masterpiece."

Tucker got to meet the players he had watched on TV regularly: Ken Caminiti, Larry Andersen, Jim Deshaies, Terry Puhl, Craig Reynolds, Kevin Bass. Puhl had pine tar on his batting glove when he shook hands. "Oooh," Tucker said. "We don't use that stuff."

He also met Astros manager Art Howe. And broadcasters Bill Worrell, Larry Dierker, and Enos Cabell, and General Manager Bill Wood.

But Tucker's real thrill was meeting Doran, the Astros' hustling second baseman. "I play second base, too," Tucker told Doran. "Started at third base. They moved me to center field and then to second."

Before the game, Doran played a game of pepper with Tucker—the kid with cerebral palsy throwing the ball and Doran slapping it back. Once Tucker made a diving catch, just as his hero had done many times before.

"You're a left-handed second baseman?" the Astros catcher Craig Biggio asked. "How do you turn double plays?"

"We don't turn any double plays," Tucker replied.

Pitcher Larry Andersen looked at the bat Doran gave Tucker. "See this nick on the end of it?" Andersen joked. "That's the only spot he made contact."

After Tucker threw out the first pitch to the applause of Astros fans, who leaped to their feet when they saw him take the mound, Doran told Tucker to make sure and show up for the next meeting of the Astros Orbiters, the Astros fan club. (Doran, it turned out, gave Tucker his May Player-of-the-Month plaque.)

The two have formed an extraordinary bond. In an age when the ranks of selfish, arrogant professional athletes seems to swell with each passing day, Doran maintains regular contact with Tucker even though he no longer plays in Houston. For a couple of years he played for the Cincinnati Reds, now he's with the Milwaukee Brewers. And the two still talk regularly on the phone.

What do they talk about? Family, school, baseball. "He

always wants to know if my kids are all right," Doran said. "I tell him to work harder in school, that that's going to be so important to him. I really think he's coming around now."

Doran's five feet, nine and muscular. He goes sprawling for any ball that he has even a remote chance of catching. Growing up in Cincinnati, the city of seven hills, Doran has adopted only the on-field behavior of another Cincinnati native, Pete Rose. You don't find him taking his money to the track. He either spends it on his family or on needy children.

Back problems cost Doran a chance to play in the World Series with Cincinnati. "That was nothing compared to what kids like Tucker have to go through every day," Doran said.

The thirty-one-year-old father of three, a veteran of ten years in the majors, said he and Tucker "just kind of hit it off... I really enjoy his company... I really see him as a monument of strength. Kids like him really are fighting the odds every minute, every second. We have no idea how tough these kids have to be, how tough their parents have to be... What I liked about his parents is that they didn't try to baby him, or make things comfortable for him. They treated him like every other kid. I'd like to think that I could handle a family situation as well as they have, but I don't know if I could."

Doran, who has long worked with developmentally handicapped children in Cincinnati, said that what happened to Tucker reflects the general direction of sports today. "People forget what they're teaching kids. They're just worried about winning. I see it all the time at Little League games. Every game there are two or three sets of parents screaming and yelling. The Little League officials have to find a way to control the atmosphere. You'd think it was the seventh game of the World Series. They treat kids worse than [former Chicago Bears Coach] Mike Ditka treated his quarterback Jim Harbaugh when he was yelling at him on the sideline."

Not once, Doran said, has he ever heard Tucker feeling

sorry for himself. "That's why I felt so bad for him when they were trying to kick him out of Little League. Here's a kid who probably wanted to play more than anyone else and they treat him that way."

Doran and Tucker filmed a public service spot for the United Cerebral Palsy Foundation. The video shows Tucker sliding into base with that huge smile of his on his face.

"I'll tell you how I'll always remember Tucker," said Doran. "In the commercial, I pick him up after he's slid into a base and we start talking about how you have to work together to beat cerebral palsy. Tucker could have just faked the slide. But he said if he did that, he wouldn't feel like he had just slid in. So he kept running in that run of his and sliding in over and over again until we got the commercial right. It had to have hurt him. His legs are so twisted up. But he just kept right on going."

Doran said being around Tucker has meant a lot to him, has helped him grow.

"I'm no superstar like Nolan Ryan or Pete Rose, so it really makes me feel good that he singled me out. If I've given him a boost, I'm happy. Because he's really given me one... Being close to him has made me keep things in perspective. In the past, I've kind of lost it now and then. Sometimes I take every game so seriously, and then I take it home with me to my family. After being around Tucker, I realized that you just have to give it your best and then don't complain about it. Here's a kid who would like to run and do things, and he's not able to. He helped me appreciate what I was able to do even when I didn't do it well. You might say Tucker gave me a perspective check on life."

Judi Church said that Doran and the Astros also gave Tucker a perspective check on life. "It was just another one of those things that proved to him that not everybody out there is against you because you're different. If every disabled kid could get that feeling some way, it would be wonderful."

Doran said he hoped that Little League officials also learned something positive from their experience with Tucker.

It appears that they didn't and they haven't. They're hassling the disabled to the point where the U.S. Department of Justice has had to get involved. Little League officials have tried to write a rule prohibiting coaches in wheelchairs. If a child is deaf in one ear, Little League officials want to place him or her in a special league for the handicapped—the kind of "separate but equal" thinking that the U.S. Supreme Court outlawed in education years ago.

But then what can you expect from an organization that doesn't think the death of one Little League coach at the hands of another is even worthy of discussion by the board of directors?

Chapter 10

Five years prior to Tucker's bout with unfeeling bureaucracy, Cameron Dobos had had the feeling beaten out of him by another coach, David Mark White. The lawyers for Judith Dobos—Kelli McDonald and Michael Sydow—used Tucker's experience to further zero in on the arrogance of Little League's chain of command.

Their questioning in depositions of Elmer Lehotsky, Joseph Losch, Michael Witherwax, Paul Goolsby, and Gus Benis—key national, state, and district officials in Tucker's experience—coupled with the sworn testimony of Little League president Creighton Hale, resulted in an unmistakable revelation: Little League is another American institution that is largely all form and no substance.

The depositions of Hale and his finance man, Daniel Roup, also serve to illustrate dramatically that Little League cares more about a buck than people—that the millions of dollars Little League rakes in truly aren't going to benefit America's children, but simply to make it appear that way.

Judith Dobos' original 1985 court petition spells out what happened to her husband, the forty-four-year-old father of three:

"On the evening of June 20, 1984, decedent Cameron S. Dobos was coaching his Little League baseball team at the Little League ballpark located at Cromwell and Hardy Streets in Houston, Harris County, Texas. His team was engaged in a duly scheduled game with the Little League

team from Magnolia, Texas, coached by defendant, David
Mark White. During the course of that game defendant
David Mark White became incensed and violent on several
occasions when umpiring decisions went against his team.
Defendant David Mark White became so violent over
this Little League game that Little League officials ejected
him from the park on one occasion, but subsequently
allowed him to return. Upon his return he again became
incensed when an umpiring decision went against his
team. On this occasion he ran up behind decedent
Cameron S. Dobos and struck him a violent blow,
breaking his jaw, causing cerebral hemorrhage and
ultimately death."

Judith Dobos sits in her home and shakes her head.

"I still can't believe it happened," she says, "and my
sons and I saw it happen right in front of us."

As so often happens now in a nation where violence
has become commonplace, David Mark White received
only a fine and a year's probation for the assault.

You would think, however, that a beating death on a
Little League baseball field would get the immediate
attention of the organization's top brass.

You'd expect them to at least deliver condolences to
the family.

They didn't.

When they heard that the death had taken place in
front of the Dobos family as well as other youngsters,
you'd think they'd rush psychological help in, much as
they do in schools when a tragedy occurs.

They didn't.

To try and ensure that a similar episode didn't occur,
you'd expect them to at least review training and screening
guidelines for coaches.

They didn't.

Don't think that a lack of money had anything to do
with the lack of action. According to the sworn testimony
of Little League's accountant during a court suit brought
by the Dobos family, the organization ran up millions in
surplus through the eighties, choosing to spend the

money on little-used, but fashionable "training centers" with swimming pools in such posh areas of the country as St. Petersburg, Florida, and San Bernadino, California.

Buildings, not people, are at the core of Little League president Creighton Hale's vision for the organization.

In his sworn deposition, part of the Dobos lawsuit, Hale couldn't have come off much colder. Under questioning by A. Glenn Diddell III, a colleague of McDonald and Sydow, Hale revealed that the organization has the soul of a machine:

Diddell: "...It is my understanding that the national organization has done nothing to ensure that the kind of episode that occurred with Dobos will ever happen again?"

Hale: "That is correct."

Diddell: "It has not in any way questioned the management of the Magnolia Sports Association?"

Hale: "No, we have not."

Diddell: "Didn't you feel that on the basis of what you learned about this incident that some inquiries should be made as to how Magnolia Sports Association selected its managers?"

Hale: "No."

Diddell: "It's also my understanding, on the basis of your testimony, that as of today you have never discussed the Dobos incident with the Board of Directors; is that correct?"

Hale: "That's correct. Nor any other fatality."

Diddell: "Don't you think the Board of Directors would want to know of an act of this magnitude..."

Hale: "No."

Diddell: "You don't think they would be interested in that?"

Hale: "No."

Diddell: "Why not?"

Hale: "Because that's not a policy."

Diddell: "Isn't it a policy of the Little League to stand for and propagate good sportsmanship and good conduct."

Hale: "Yes, it is."

Diddell: "And doesn't—I mean, that's what Little League represents."

Hale: "That's what we try to attain."

Diddell: "When you have mayhem on the playing field, so to speak, doesn't that create a problem for the efficacy of what Little League stands for?"

Hale: "But not of the magnitude to bring it to the board.

Diddell: "Death isn't of the magnitude to bring it to the board?"

Hale: "We don't bring any death to the board."

Diddell: "Not even criminal conduct by a manager?"

Hale: "That's correct."

Now you can understand how a Tucker Church kind of episode can so easily crop up in Little League. The sad truth is, the brass aren't people-oriented. They're bottom-line types.

Well, that's not completely true, of course. In his deposition, Little League accountant Daniel Roupp revealed that "at this complex here in Williamsport, we have a dining hall and we provide lunch free of charge to our employees." And Hale, who took over Little League's top job in 1984 at forty-five thousand dollars, has more than doubled his beginning salary. Think of it: a hundred grand, a free car, and first-class air travel around the world—all for telling Little League volunteers across the country that they have all the answers, not his paid staff.

Except, of course, when the disabled are involved.

It's also true that Hale cares a lot about Dan Quayle. In 1990 Hale fell all over himself as he gushed about Dan Quayle's induction into the Little League Hall of Excellence.

To his credit, Hale didn't burst into his rendition of "Danny Boy."

"Vice President Quayle," Hale said, "was selected for this prestigious distinction on his qualifications as a leader, role model for children, and his commitment to excellence."

Now Hale could have inducted Cameron Dobos and Tucker Church into the Little League Hall of Excellence, too. But, of course, he wouldn't have gotten to meet the vice president of the United States. Dobos coached Little League for fourteen years and ultimately gave his life working with kids. That's one heckuva role model. His local Little League, at least, did name the field after him.

As for Tucker, well, even Jim Ferguson, the director of Little League's three-year-old Challenger program, which provides baseball for the disabled, concedes he played a huge role in causing the program to grow from less than three hundred kids in 1989 to the more than twenty-five thousand who are playing today.

You can bet Dobos' family would have appreciated the recognition and attention. Especially Cameron Dobos' youngest son, Jonathan. He was in the third grade when he watched his father get beaten to death.

During questioning by Terry Fry, the attorney for Little League's insurance company, Jonathan Dobos told how his father's death affected him:

Fry: "I found out in your mom's deposition when she went through this about a year and a half ago that you had some problems after your father's death, correct?"

Jonathan: "Correct."

Fry: "I think your mom said something about you decided that you wanted to go be with your dad and that you locked yourself up in the car or something?"

Jonathan: "Yes, correct."

Fry: "And you thought that if you locked yourself up in the car, you would join your father?"

Jonathan: "Yes."

Fry: "Did your mom take you to the doctor after that?"

Jonathan: "Psychiatrist."

Fry: "Can you tell me, aside from this incident that we've just talked about, how the loss of your father has affected you?"

Jonathan: "…Well, there's a lot of things I hadn't done yet since I was very young. Like he went with me on my first airplane flight and everything. There's just a lot of stuff he didn't get to do with me."

It is unconscionable that Hale, on behalf of his organization, did not immediately see what he could do to help the Dobos family.

Why would the head of Little League baseball, who's forever espousing family values in the organization's literature, fail to contact the wife of a man who had coached kids for fourteen years? Why didn't he see if there was anything he could do for the children? Why can he fly off to Japan on a public relations' jaunt but not to Houston when a Little League coach gets beaten to death in front of children?

What is also disturbing in the Dobos case is the treatment afforded Cameron Dobos' eldest son, Cameron Todd Dobos, by Little League baseball. After having coached eight- and nine-year-olds from 1982 to 1987, he suddenly was told in 1988 he couldn't coach any more. That timing, according to attorney Kelli McDonald, coincided with increased court action in the case.

Little League's attorney Terry Fry asked Cameron Todd Dobos about his relationship with the organization during a 1990 deposition.

Fry: "What leagues did you coach for?"

Dobos: "North Houston American Little League."

Fry: "Always the same league?"

Dobos: "Yeah."

Fry: "And have you coached since '87?"

Dobos: "No."

Fry: "Why not?"

Dobos: "In 1988, we had signed up—I had signed up to coach a team again, and I was told by the president of the league that I was not going to be able to coach."

Fry: "Who told you that?"

Dobos: "Mr. Don Diaz."

Fry: "Did he tell you anything other than you were not able to coach?"

Dobos: "He never gave a specific reason, no."

Fry: "What sort of personal thing was there between you and Mr. Diaz?"

Dobos: "Me and Mr. Diaz, we had been good friends. As a matter of fact, him and my father were best of friends, and he had approached my mother after the incident [his dad's death] wanting to know if she thought it would be nice on behalf of my father if he ran for president. We thought it was a great idea because we were good friends with him."

Fry: "'He' being Mr. Diaz?"

Dobos: "Right. So he decided to run that year because my father was going to run for president of the office that year of his death. And Mr. Diaz ran, and he did win, and he remained president for five years. The whole time he had asked me to be on his board, and I did, and I was elected. I served on his board, coached for several years out there after my father's incident, and then, all of a sudden in 1988 everything just turned cold as ice."

Fry: "And no one ever gave you any explanation as to why you were not allowed to coach?"

Dobos: "That's right. We had called him on the phone several times. He wouldn't talk with us. He would hang up on us. We sent him a certified letter requesting him to at least write and tell us what his problem was and what—you know, what kind of thing he had on us. Never heard any response from him."

Fry: "Do you have any other idea as to why you're not allowed to coach by Mr. Diaz?"

Dobos: "I have my own idea, yes."

Fry: "What's that?"

Dobos: "The fact that about this time was when we— our family—had started pressing on with the case, it was about 1988. At that time, from what I get, he must have gotten orders from somebody in Little League not to allow us to play or to coach out there anymore."

Fry: "Some orders from my client in Williamsport, Pennsylvania?"

Dobos: "In that it happened after we coached three years with no problem out there after the incident, and all of a sudden when the case started coming to a head, then all of a sudden they wouldn't let us coach anymore."

Fry: "Do you have any information, has anybody told you, have you read anything, do you have any information that points, that is, in fact, to what happened; that is, that someone from my client, Little League Baseball Inc., contacted someone or in some way was involved in your not being allowed to coach by Mr. Diaz?"

Dobos: "Well, when you can't get an answer from somebody, I mean, I don't—I mean, we had been best of friends, and all of a sudden it's totally different from that point on, you have to suspect something has happened."

To this day, Dobos has never been given an explanation of why he was kicked out of coaching Little League. Nor has anyone been able to tell me why he was. It is not uncommon, however, for businesses who have been sued by someone to stop doing business with that individual. What is so tragic in this case is that the younger Dobos was considered an excellent coach by everyone in Little League. If Little League did act like many other businesses—and its callousness would suggest that it may well have—and play hardball with Dobos, the children came away the big losers. You hear from people then connected with the North Houston American Little League—former coaches like Alfred Luna—who says the younger Dobos was a fine coach, just like his father.

How big a hand did Creighton Hale have in the Dobos case? No one knows for sure. But anybody close to Little League Baseball says that the sixty-nine-year-old Hale *is* Little League Baseball. What he says goes. "He's the man," says Houston district administrator Paul Goolsby.

Hale was born February 18, 1924, in Hardy, Nebraska. He attended the University of Nebraska for one year before entering the Navy. After three years and service in World War II, he was honorably discharged as an ensign. He received his bachelor's degree in liberal arts from

Colgate University in Hamilton, New York, in 1949. He then entered Springfield College in Springfield, Massachusetts, to pursue a master's degree in physical education. Ask him if Springfield is nationally known for its physical education program and he replies: "Internationally known."

After receiving his master's, he joined the Springfield faculty, where he stayed until leaving to become Little League Baseball's director of research in 1955. Shortly thereafter he received his Ph.D. from New York University in education. His dissertation topic, in the field of physiology, was a study on the energy consumption of carrying the infantry pack. It wasn't published.

He remained Little League's director of research, and added the duties of assistant to the president and vice-president, before becoming president of Little League Baseball in 1973. He also became chief executive officer. In addition to the titles of president and chief executive, Hale is a member of Little League's board of directors and the board's investment committee as well a member of Little League Baseball's charter and rules committees. He has also served as secretary-treasurer of the Little League Foundation, a separate corporation and funding organization for Little League.

Since he's been with Little League Baseball for thirty-eight years and now has a position of power in every meaningful administrative area, it's not surprising that many connected with the organization think that what he says is gospel.

Interviewed in January 1993, Hale had no explanation for his startling coldness in the wake of the Dobos tragedy. He bristled when asked if callousness had been institutionalized under his leadership of Little League. "I really have got nothing to say," he said. He made it clear he didn't want to talk about either the Dobos or Church affair. Nor did he want to talk about his organization's insensitivity toward the disabled. "I've got to go," he said.

If, as one lawyer suggested, Hale didn't show any

compassion for the Dobos family because of the fear of possible litigation, then Americans have to wonder if Little League baseball would be better off without him. Is that an example we want our children to live by? Doesn't human life have to be more important than the fear of losing a buck? Besides, you're not admitting any kind of guilt by expressing sorrow, by saying how much a man had meant to an organization.

Jonathan Dobos, who was so upset by his father's death that he had to repeat the third grade, wrote a story about his father's death that his mother sent to Little League headquarters. There was never a reply. This is what he wrote at age nine:

CAMERON DOBOS' STORY

"On June the 20th 1984, a very bad accident happened at North Houston American Little League. My dad, Cameron Dobos, was coaching sixteen, seventeen, and eighteen-year-olds... when the accident happened. The teams were the North Houston Pirates which Cameron Dobos was coaching at the time. Cameron was coaching third base when the man from the other team, Magnolia Rebels, was complaining about the pitcher being illegal. You see, the first game they played the pitcher was not there but (the) second he was. He was pitching a no hitter. The score was five to one. My dad's team was winning. The Magnolia coach was a hothead. He had forgot it was a kid's game. He had went into the dugout. He picked up something and hit my dad. He was taken to Parkway Hospital. They couldn't do anything so he was flew by Life Flight from Parkway to Hermann Hospital. That's where he died. He passed away on July 1, 1984. The funeral was on July 3, 1984. Jonathan Dobos, age nine, I am the youngest child of Cameron Dobos. Because of a hothead coach three boys are without a dad today. This story was written on July 13, 1984, which is Cameron Dobos birthday. We all love you dad."

The remaining members of the Dobos family are classic

examples of survivor victims. Each is struggling to get over what they saw play out before them. Judith Dobos knows all too well that her husband can't relate the terror and pain that he suffered, that he can't protest that he was denied the most fundamental right of all—the right to life. She feels it, and tries to protest for him, but she's been paralyzed by the futility of it all and has remained virtually housebound since Cameron's death. Her children have seen her go into a shell, and they worry about her even as they try to deal with their own grief. For the living victims of a violent death, there is no parole. Their life sentence is to live with the fact that their loved one died at the hands of another human being.

"I just wish for other people's sake, so nobody else had to go through this, that Little League would try and screen coaches," Judith Dobos says. "And there should have been mandatory training so these guys have some idea of how to deal with their feelings."

Larry Roberts, who was the North American Little League president when Cameron was beaten to death, wrote a letter to Little League headquarters. He pleaded for help. None came.

In the letter Roberts pointed out that ten days after Dobos was beaten, another manager took several swings at an umpire. When the umpire slipped, the manager kicked him. Roberts said he removed the man "from managing his ten-year-old tournament team" and would "leave a letter to this effect for the 1985 Executive Board and President...

"...My question to you is how are we supposed to keep people with uncontrollable tempers out of Little League? What is to keep these people from leaving one ballpark and going to another?"

They were good questions, particularly since David Mark White, after beating Dobos, ended up as an umpire in another Houston-area Little League for two years.

"I'm sorry the accident happened," White said in January 1993. "I spent a little time in jail, did my probation, and paid a fine. I paid my debt to society. And

I did a good job umpiring out in Tomball, too. I'm hoping to manage again soon."

Under Creighton Hale's leadership of Little League, it could happen. Unless, of course, White was found to be disabled. Then Hale would most likely take action to remove him from the playing field. Hale likes to say everything is a local Little League's concern, it seems, unless it's a question about the disabled. A death doesn't interest him, doesn't make him concerned about safety, doesn't make him search for a solution to the growing tide of mayhem on the Little League playing field. But for some reason when the disabled are involved, he gets all hot and bothered about safety.

Hale doesn't want to spend Little League money to train and screen coaches to help ensure that what happened to Cameron Dobos doesn't happen again, but he doesn't mind spending money in court battling lawsuits filed because there is no standard of training that must be met. Sure, coaches are volunteers, as the Little League brass are fond of saying. They use that as an argument against any mandatory training and screening. But volunteer firemen are volunteers, too, and they receive mandatory training. So do volunteer deputies. Because someone is a volunteer deputy, are you going to let him roam the street with a gun and no training? Should we just give over our children to a coach like David Mark White, or Bob Whitfill, the man who first gave Tucker Church such a hard time? Don't we want to see that everything possible within reason is done to get men of high values and moral character as coaches?

Don't think that what happened to Dobos is too much of an aberration on the Little League playing field. Consider the following:

• In 1991 Little League Coach Steven Fuller was convicted by a Clark County Superior Court jury of second-degree assault with a deadly weapon for hitting an umpire with a baseball bat during a post-game argument in Vancouver, Washington.

• Houston Little League Umpire Ben Vaughn said he's

seen his colleagues beaten so severely that they suffered broken jawbones.

• In July 1990, John Hills of Lemont, Illinois, was coaching first base for the thirteen-, fourteen-, and fifteen-year-old Senior League All-stars when he was attacked by a rival coach and players. They didn't like him talking to an umpire about calls made at first base. By the time it was over, Hills had several broken ribs, a broken nose, a ruptured spleen, a lacerated kidney, and a grapefruit-sized bruise behind his knee where he had been struck with a bat. He spent ten days in the hospital. His assailants were convicted of misdemeanors and given community service time.

"My wife saw it happen to me and I think she's really been affected," Hills said. "I think all the kids were, too. We were very, very lucky that kids didn't get involved in this. They could have been killed."

Once again, Little League's national headquarters did not offer any counseling to the youngsters or Hills' family. Nor did Little League offer any condolences, although headquarters did send someone to investigate liability questions.

For seven years, the attorneys for Dobos tried to get Little League to hand over its files on coaches assaulting other coaches, striking young players or abusing minors. Little League stonewalled.

Court records show that Hale was supposed to bring with him to his deposition all documents relating to claims against Little League Baseball that had arisen out of the activities of coaches over a ten-year period. Hale appeared at his deposition without the documentation. Asked where it was, he said the chief financial officer, Daniel Roupp, had it. When Roupp appeared for his deposition, he said he no longer had custody of the documents, that the insurance carriers did. When representatives of the insurance carriers showed up, many did not bring the documents. The one who did, refused to allow Dobos' attorneys to inspect the documents.

Little League attorneys finally settled with the Dobos

family for $1.2 million in 1991 rather than turn over the documents. That means America's parents don't know just how much at risk their children are.

Mandating screening and training of coaches and putting a mechanism in place so hotheads can never get back into the organization—which may save the lives of youngsters or coaches—still isn't something Hale wants to spend time or money on. Better to put up some buildings or "training centers" at five regional centers that few ever use. According to sworn testimony of Little League's accountant, less than two thousand kids each year use the camps at the training centers that cost millions to build. And then the kids must pay to use them. According to Hale's sworn testimony, few coaches use them for training. The facilities do look really professional, however. They even have pools.

Form without substance, that's Hale's Little League.

True, many Little League games are played on the fields at the training facilities. But they could still have been played at existing ball fields. Little League isn't the kind of organization that needs a Cadillac-level facility when an existing Chevrolet-style ball field does just fine.

It's not really a stretch to think that Hale's callousness begets callousness throughout the organization. The man at the top always sets the tone. When caring and compassion aren't cornerstones of an enterprise, you can easily end up with a Tucker Church episode. Perhaps, if action had been taken by Little League when the first violence occurred on Little League playing fields, Cameron Dobos would have been alive today. Maybe if David Mark White had even been asked if there was any violence in his background, he would have told Little League officials that his wife had filed a complaint against him for allegedly beating her. While court documents show she declined to press charges later, at least Little League would have had an inkling that he might have temper problems.

Perhaps then, officials could have acted with caution.

It was only after Cameron Dobos' niece, attorney Kelli McDonald, learned of Little League's behavior toward her uncle that a suit was filed. "I just couldn't believe that a guy who donated so much time to kids would be treated just like he was a piece of dirt," McDonald says.

Alfred Luna, a fellow coach of Dobos, was stunned by the national organization's behavior.

"I just couldn't believe that they didn't send someone down to talk to the family," he said. "They were acting as if coaches get killed every day on the playing field. And this was a coach who was running for president of the league when he was killed. He was very well-liked. He never got in fights or argued. He was all out for the kids. I'm sure he would have won president. I made treasurer that year.

At least we got the local field named for him. I felt good about that."

Tucker Church, who was surprised to have learned that he and Dobos will be linked forever through a court case, seemed stunned by Hale's treatment of the Dobos family and his reluctance to at least attempt to get good coaches.

"You wonder sometimes," Tucker says, "how people who don't really seem to care about people get where they do."

What is so curious is that in their official rule book, Little League officials appear to understand the importance to children of good managers—men like Cameron Dobos and Scott Davis. They appear to want men who would never do what was done to Tucker Church or Cameron Dobos.

In reality, however, Hale and his boys pay only lip service to what is written by the late Dr. Arthur A. Esslinger under the heading of "Little League's Greatest Challenge."

Esslinger wrote:

"The heart of Little League Baseball is what happens between the manager and the player. It is your manager more than any other single individual who makes your program a success or failure. He controls the situation in

which players may be benefited or harmed. We have all
seen managers who exerted a wonderful influence upon
their players—an influence which was as fine an
educational experience as any youngster might undergo.
Unfortunately, we have also observed a few managers
who were a menace to children...

"My contention is that from the league president's
point of view, your manager is the most important
volunteer in the Little League program. A variety of
reasons support this contention. A very important factor
is the youngster of Little League age wants to emancipate
himself from his primary identification with his parent...

"The child now seeks for other persons to typify the
ideals and virtues that once used to be represented by the
parents. This is an age of hero worship. If a child chooses
as a model an adult who represents the highest ideals of
gentlemanly behavior and clean living both the child
and his parents are fortunate...

"We have stimulated the imagination of millions of
youngsters to come into this program. Yet for their
leadership we have largely trusted to the luck of the
draw—to mere accident. The least we can do for all these
youngsters is to try to find them a good manager and
once selected provide him with some indoctrination and
in-service training. This, it seems to me is a solemn
obligation. The quality of leadership represents our biggest
problem and until we solve it we can never realize the
full potential we have."

To even the most casual reader, it has to sound like
Esslinger is proposing mandatory training. Poor managers,
Esslinger wrote, are the greatest threat to the Little League
program. You can bet John Hills believes that. And
Cameron Dobos' widow and children, too. In another
article entitled "Manager" that appeared in an official
Little League publication, Esslinger wrote: "While an adult
with training and background in the game is a desirable
candidate for manager and coach, league screen
committees should look for other important qualities."

Hale tried to distance himself from both of Esslinger's writings during his deposition in the Dobos case. On the question of screening committees he got testy during questioning by attorney Diddell. He attempted to say that what Esslinger wrote regarding screening committees was only a recommendation.

Diddell: "I don't see the word "recommendation" in that paragraph. Do you?"

Hale: "No."

Diddell: "What is your understanding of the function of the league screening committee as it's discussed here?"

Hale: "There's no league screening committee."

Diddell: "What are they talking about?"

Hale: "I don't know what he's talking about. He's not even one of our staff people. He was on the board of directors. Professional physical education man who wrote this as a guide for Little League, but it's not a document which is implemented as such from headquarters.

Diddell: "Well, it's part of your manual, correct?"

Hale: "Part of the manual."

Diddell: "And it's written… as part of the text of the manual under "Manager."

Hale: "Right."

Diddell: "And these, as I understand it, are guidelines for the selection of managers by the local organizations… what's in this book?"

Hale: "Well, yes… but the fact of the matter is, even though it's in there, there are no screening committees… We got something in there that doesn't belong… it will come out…"

So instead of committing his organization to trying to weed out the bad apples with more vigor than ever, Hale does the opposite. He remains committed to what Esslinger referred to as "the luck of the draw." And yet this is a man who continually says he's concerned about safety and how managers and Little League personnel can affect the lives of children. If the Dobos tragedy sent a message, it's that the selection of good managers is a definite safety concern. If the Tucker Church affair sent a message about managers, it's that a good one like Scott Davis should be held in high esteem, not vilified. Hale didn't get either message.

Hale tried to say that headquarters could do nothing to make Esslinger's proposal for training coaches come true. The following exchanges are revealing in how little emphasis Little League actually places on training coaches:

Diddell: Would you assume it (Esslinger's guideline for managers) would be something you would hope... local organizations would read and consider?

Hale: "We could only hope that."

Diddell: Okay. Isn't that a reasonable expectation on your part?

Hale: "Not necessarily, with the amount of time that the volunteer has..."

Diddell: "...The national organization does have a training program for managers, is that correct?"

Hale: "For those that are able to take part in it, which is a very low percentage of the total."

Diddell: "...Would you expect that there would be a record of training sessions in the training director's office?"

Hale: "No."

Diddell: "Do you keep any records of the number of training seminars that are given?"

Hale: "No."

Diddell: How do you memorialize, if you memorialize, feedback that you get during those sessions?

Hale: "We don't. Just staff meeting that's reported."

Diddell: "Does the staff consolidate what transpires in those session into any written format?"

Hale: "No."

Diddell: "Do you modify the manual according to the feedback that you get?"

Hale: "Not particularly, no."

Diddell: Do you know if it has ever been modified on the basis of feedback from the field?"

Hale: "Probably not."

Player with cerebral palsy joins coach in defying league ban

By JULIE MASON
Houston Chronicle

Ben DeSoto / /Chronicle

Tucker Church, 15, is carried off the field by fellow players Friday night after his Little League game. The 4-foot-9, 59-pound centerfielder with cerebral palsy has played on a team of 9 to 12-year-olds since he was13 but was told by officials last week that he was too old.

Tucker hurch played baseball Friday night, defying an order from Little League officials banning him from the field.

And his coach, Scott Davis — who was told by the same officials he could never coach in any league again because he allowed Tucker, 15, to play baseball with younger kids — was there in the dugout, cheering on Tucker and the Pirates.

Tucker, a 4-foot 9-inch, 59-pound centerfielder with cerebral palsy, has played a team of 9- to 12-year-olds since he was 13, said his mother, Judi Church. And then a complaint from a team competing with the Pirates for second place in the league prompted officials to force Tucker from the team and request the resignation of the coach who let him play.

"These kids are just here to have fun. If the adults would just leave them alone, they'd be fine," she said.

Among Tucker Church's supporters at the last game of the season Friday night was Adrienne Lyons, a mother with two deaf sons, Charles, 12 and Daniel, 11, on the opposing team.

"We're all out here for the boys, and no one thinks of any of these kids as deficient in any way," she said. "If it wasn't for some grown-ups getting greedy for trophies, there wouldn't be any problem."

Tucker's father, Terry, who cheered the Pirates from the bleachers Friday night, said playing baseball has given his son self-confidence he may not have gotten anywhere else.

"It's all politics here. Those people don't care about Tucker," he said. "He just loves the game."

The Churches this spring allowed Tucker to try out for a team of boys his own age, but said they were relieved when he didn't make the roster and Davis invited him to play for the Pirates.

"One of those kids was named 'Beef,'" Tucker's mother said. "He can't play with those kids, he's so small."

She said Tucker didn't mind playing on the younger kids' team. "He just loves to play."

Sandy Davis, wife of the beleaguered coach, said her husband was more upset about Tucker not being able to play baseball next year than he was about being banned from coaching.

But she added, Little League officials told Davis that their son, Sean, who will be eligible to play baseball next year, is also banned from the league.

"We really feel like Sharpstown is behind us 120 percent, but I'm angry about what (national league officials are) doing to these kids," she said.

No league officials attended the game Friday night, and none could be reached for comment.

Terry Church said Tucker came to play Friday with two doctors' letters and a waiver from their insurance company stating that if Tucker were injured in the game, his family would not sue the league.

"It's still not good enough for them," he said. "Why do they have to turn Little League into a dictatorship?"

Lyons said she is concerned league officials may start a "disabled" league next year.

"They don't need a league like that. These kids need to play together," she said.

"If they make Tucker leave, if he wasn't here, then all the boys who played on his team and all the boys who played against him would have missed out on knowing him and seeing his determination and his inner strength. And that would be a shame."

Sherry Simoneaux, the wife of Sharpstown Little League president Lercy Simoneaux, said the decisions regarding Tucker and his coach have disillusioned league officials.

"You better believe they have supporters," she said of Tucker and his coach.

Across the dugout, in the bleachers of the opposing team, the A's, parents waved homemade signs declaring their support for Davis.

Credit: Michael Boddy, *The Houston Post*

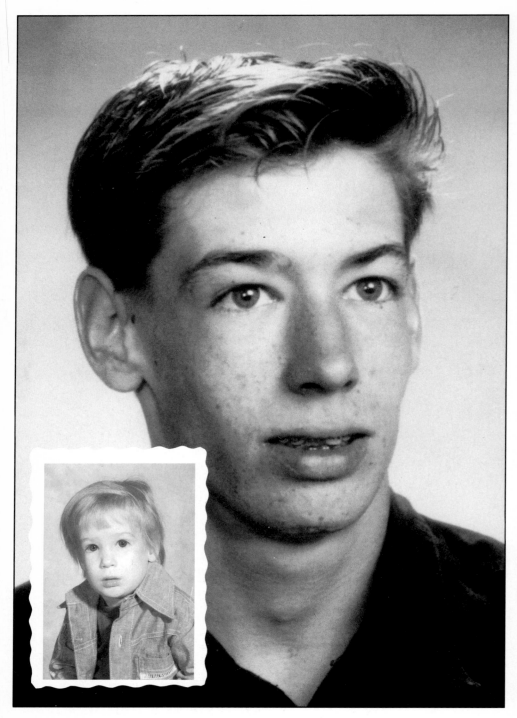

Tucker at one year of age [inset] in Bridgeport, Connecticut. At seventeen, this is how he appeared in the program guide for the Million Dollar Roundtable. He spoke before the prestigious group of insurance executives in 1992.
Credit: The Church collection

Four-year-old Tucker sits by a
hotel swimming pool in Houston.
Credit: The Church collection

Santa Claus with Tucker, six, and
Tucker's sister Marriah, two.
Credit: The Church collection

When he was ten, Tucker occasionally
rode Elvira, his sister Marriah's horse.
Credit: The Church collection

Tucker at eighteen in the motor
home that the Church family
used on a camping trip.
Credit: The Church collection

During his Little League career, Tucker played for the Pirates at fifteen, the A's at ten, and the Rams at seven.
Credit: Bruce Bennet, *The Houston Post*
Credit [insets]: The Church collection

TUCKER CHURCH
SHARPSTOWN LITTLE LEAGUE

ASTROS

1987
SEASON CHAMPS

Manager

1987
TOURNAMENT CHAMPS

Tucker's Little League team won the Sharpstown
Little League Championship in 1987.
Credit: The Church collection

Tucker with former Houston Astros Billy
Doren. Doren, now with the Milwaukee
Brewers, became a close friend of Tucker's
after his run-in with Little League in 1989.
Credit: The Church collection

Tucker goes to bat in Palermo, New York, after he was invited to be the special guest of the Palermo Youth Organization. Also shown are his Houston coach, Scott Davis, umpiring, and Palermo's John Chmielewski catching. *Credit: Terry Bennet*

Nick Sterio, the Palermo, New York, man who first suggested that Tucker be a guest of the Palermo Youth Organization, shakes Tucker's hand after he hit a home run. *Credit: Terry Bennet*

Each Member of the Palermo, New York, Youth Organization chipped in to buy Tucker a "Most Valuable Player" trophy. He's shown here with [left to right] Palermo's Nick Sterio, Tucker's coach Scott Davis, and Palermo's Alona Kalin and David Redhead. *Credit: Terry Bennet*

Tucker shows off his new trophy to members of the Palermo Youth Organization. *Credit: Terry Bennet*

After his battle with Little League, Tucker was asked to be a guest disc jockey on Houston radio station, KODA. The station even advertised his debut [lower]. Tucker [upper, center] is shown here [left to right] with program director David McKay, DJ Brent Clanton, and general manager Dusty Black.
Credit: The Church collection

Everett Evans, the Imperial Potentate of the Shriners, joins Tucker and Clint Faulkner (the Shriner who saw to it that Tucker got help) during a 1992 tour of the Houston Shriners Hospital. *Credit: Fred Howard*

Tucker often likes to return to Houston Shriners Hospital to visit with the staff. He's shown here with [left to right] nurses Elizabeth Ivey and Jane Miller.
Credit: Fred Howard

Kathleen Price is the Shriners Hospital physical therapist who helped Tucker with his painful rehabilitation
Credit: Fred Howard

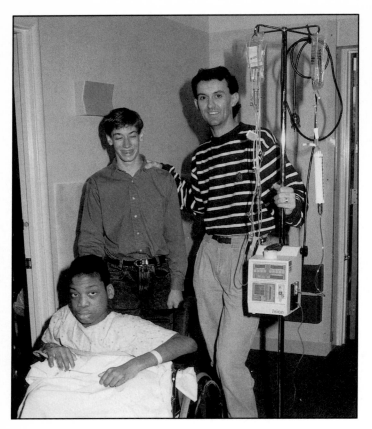

Tucker visits with [left to right] Derick Thomas, a patient at the Shriners Hospital in Houston, and Shriners staffer, Scott Davis.
Credit: Fred Howard

David McMahan, who made Tucker's braces at the Shriners Hospital, is shown with Tucker and his mother, Judi Church.
Credit: Fred Howard

Tucker and his mother, Judi, hold the braces he wore after his operations at the Shriners Hospital in Houston.
Credit: Fred Howard

Tucker shows how he practiced walking with the aid of rehabilitation equipment at the Shriners Hospital.
Credit: Fred Howard

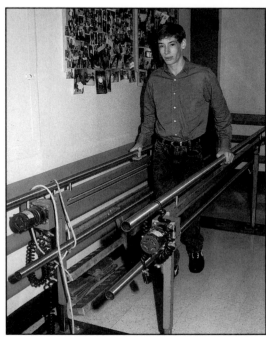

Tucker digs in the yard of his Alvin home, in 1992.
Credit: The Church collection

Tucker often uses the family's tractor to work in the yard.
Credit: The Church collection

Tucker does his Arnold Schwarzenegger imitation.
Credit: The Church collection

Tucker, who never expected to be able to drive because of his cerebral palsy, is all smiles in 1992 after he got his driver's license.
Credit: The Church collection

Little League officials, then, don't learn from their mistakes, nor do they care to try. They couldn't seem to care less if those who forget their history are condemned to repeat it. Their attitude suggests that if a lawsuit results because they've refused to act responsibly and change course, why should they get uptight? It's not their money that goes down the drain. If somebody dies, just don't bring it up at the board of directors' meeting. If some children aren't as mentally tough as Tucker Church and their psyches get scarred from the same kind of offensive adult behavior he endured, why worry? Most children do just fine in Little League, thank you.

If Little League Baseball Inc., which was founded in 1939 and federally chartered in 1963, sounds more like a stone-cold business than a children-first enterprise, that's because it is. Daniel Roupp's testimony in a 1990 deposition taken by Michael Sydow and Kelli McDonald, the attorneys for the Dobos family, proved that.

The deposition was taken in Williamsport, Pennsylvania, the international headquarters of Little League Baseball, where Carl Stotz began the Little League concept.

Roupp used the year 1989 to show how the money flows into Little League headquarters. He explained that for each league to affiliate with Little League they must pay a fee, called a charter fee, to the corporation. If a league doesn't have a charter, it's not part of Little League. Little League now has more than sixteen thousand chartered leagues.

In 1989, Roupp noted that Little League received more than $1.2 million in charter fees. Another $218,751 came to the organization from softball leagues that wanted to be affiliated with Little League. Little League also got $622,839 from the sale of copyrighted supplies—which include "extra" rule books for leagues that have already paid their charter fees. Little League also received $420,187 from royalties and license fees, money that generally comes from sporting good manufacturers who want to use the name "Little League." Local leagues also paid $504,698 for insurance that they must carry, although they need not purchase it from Little League. Radio and TV rights to Little League games brought in $45,729. Concession sales at tournament games brought in $407,225. Five summer camps across the country netted $679,902. Corporate sponsorships brought in another $878,560.

The total revenue generated for 1989, Roupp said, amounted to $6,723,855. Operating expenses were $5,077,043. So the non-profit corporation brought in a surplus of $1,320,529. From 1981 through 1989, the surplus amounted to $5,231,161.

Attorney Sydow asked Roupp what happened to the surpluses.

"...We made capital additions, capital improvements, and we changed that money from a cash asset to other assets," Roupp said. "There are also times when that money is left over that it's kept in the form of cash and then, possibly it could be invested or it could be used for purchases."

In other words, Tucker Church and millions of other youngsters never got to benefit from it.

When Sydow asked what other kind of assets the money gets changed into, Roupp replied: "Primarily capital assets such as buildings, equipment, property."

So more than five million dollars in surplus went into buildings, not children. A big chunk of that money, according to Roupp, went for the construction of camps at five regional Little League centers, those at San Bernadino, California; St. Petersburg, Florida; Waco, Texas; and Indianapolis, Indiana.

According to Roupp, then, millions were spent to build facilities that, by his own figures, only 1,943 children used in 1989. And then they have to pay to use them, even though most of Little League's monies are generated from the kids.

How does the Little League brass spend the money that pours in? Roupp ticked it off: salaries, field retainers, contributions to the employee retirement plan, hospitalization insurance and other benefits for employees, postage, office supplies, telephone, insurance for corporate protection, professional services, public relations, travel, feeding and housing, equipment, printing supplies, Little League Museum contributions, and development expense.

Little League employees don't have to contribute to their own retirement plan, a nice fringe benefit in troubled economic times and particularly sweet for employees who work for a non-profit company. And, oh yes, the fifty-one employees at national headquarters always get a free lunch, which proves there is such a thing as a free lunch. If, of course, the kids and their parents pay for it.

Hale makes a six-figure salary and also gets a free car. Gross salaries for eighty-one Little League personnel came to $1,466,237 in 1989. Little League spent another $397,151 on contributions to the employees' retirement and hospitalization and insurance plans. Another $386,613 was spent on vehicle and field and housing maintenance. Roupp said Little League has a fleet of thirty cars, some of which are used for employees' personal use when their own cars break down.

By the way, no money was spent to screen Little League coaches. And no money was spent to train them.

Roupp said local Little Leagues who want to sell Little League stickers for fundraising purposes must buy the stickers from national headquarters, which marks up the item over and above the cost that headquarters pays the manufacturer.

Out of all the millions that Little League headquarters take in, what do the local Little Leagues receive in return?

Hale responded in his deposition that "one operating manual is sent to each league" and a number of rule books as well, but he didn't know how many. He said umpire manuals, a safety publication, and brochures about the program are also provided, but he didn't know how many. There are training "opportunities," nothing mandatory.

That's what is given in return for millions—a rule book

that costs Little League about thirty-two cents, and a few
other publications. Unbelievable. Of course, the kids that
make it to the World Series get treated grandly, but that
only involves forty players.

In reality, Little League Baseball Inc., is just a self-
perpetuating corporation for eighty-one employees, a gravy
train for people at the home office. They can enjoy free lunches
and free trips to their regional centers around the country.

While Hale argues repeatedly that Little League is set
up as an organization run at the local level, he is quick to
point out that the charter committee at headquarters can
pull a league's charter—throw teams out of Little League—
if they don't follow guidelines handed down from
Williamsport. Couple that power with the fact that
millions of dollars are paid from the local leagues each
year to affiliate with the national organization and you're
hard pressed to see how local leagues really are in control.

All that is received for the millions forked over to
Williamsport is the Little League structure, which probably
generates more political struggles than a league truly locally
controlled. If the Sharpstown Little League had been locally
controlled, there would never have been a Tucker Church
affair. The Sharpstown board approved his playing
unanimously. Of course, the millions of dollars given to
Williamsport also give youngsters the dream of possibly
going to the World Series. And, oh yes, doling out the
millions to Williamsport gives people the joy of watching
Hale and others decide how many more millions should be
spent on the museum and other buildings few get to use.

The truth is, the vast majority of kids would want
what Tucker Church wanted. Some honest-to-goodness
baseball instruction from friendly coaches. There's no
reason with the money Little League rakes in that
opportunities can't be made for college baseball coaches
to hold clinics for kids a couple of times a year. Come to
think of it, the coaches just may donate their time. As it
stands now, a good many Little League coaches don't
know anything more about baseball than they do about
quantum physics. Likewise, money could be put down

for the screening and training of coaches—if the organization couldn't get it donated—so mothers and fathers and sons and daughters don't have to worry about their loved ones getting killed on the playing field.

John Hills, the coach who was beaten so badly by another coach in Illinois, said there is no question that Little League has to do more than just send out rule books in the future.

"We have to get mandatory training and screening for coaches," Hills said.

Harris County (Texas) Precinct 6 Constable Victor Trevino, who recently started Little Leagues in Houston areas where there haven't been any for more than twenty years, suggests that Little League headquarters spend some money promoting Little Leagues in the inner city.

"I think an organization like that has a moral obligation to help get things started where kids have few sports opportunities," he said. "Many of the parents in the inner city simply don't have any idea of how to get it started. Once officials let them know how to do it, many more leagues would start. Our kids need something like that. I would think that Little League would want to really get involved so that kids in big cities across the country don't end up burning cities like they did in Los Angeles. I've talked to lawmen and community leaders across the United States, and they feel the same way. They want to see a federal chartered organization that's making millions do something for all children, not just those out in the suburbs."

As it stands now, the Little League brass want to take the money from local leagues but don't want to accept any of the responsibility for what goes on there. Obviously, the strategy's not working, not when you pay out more than a million dollars to a family whose breadwinner was killed on the playing field.

Tucker Church believes kids would be better off if they played baseball in a youth organization similar to the one in Palermo, New York. Given his experience there, it's not difficult to understand why.

Chapter 11

The town of Palermo, New York, a small town of thirty-two hundred, sits about ten miles from Lake Ontario. Ask Tom Savage, the town supervisor, what Palermo is most famous for and he replies in one word—"Snow."

"We got six feet in one day in 1992," Savage said. "Being around the lake always gives us a lot."

Outdoorsmen are fond of the Palermo area because of the deer hunting and fishing. Motorists often find themselves waiting as a farmer walks his cows across the road. Until the mid-eighties, children carved out a field in a farmer's pasture when they wanted to play baseball. Now there's a town park with three baseball fields that always seem to be in use by the Palermo Youth Organization. When snowfall begins in October and doesn't end until May, you want to play as much as you can while you can.

What made the people of Palermo decide practically en masse—after reading a May 1989 newspaper article on Little League's treatment of a disabled Texas boy—that they must fly him and his family to their community for four days? How is it that they cared so much about what happened to a complete stranger named Tucker Church that they felt compelled to show their support? Why did they decide that what happened to Tucker Church meant they had to protest the treatment of the handicapped? All they know is that the Tucker Church affair made them mad as hell and they saw no reason for him or anybody like him to have to take it anymore. No, they didn't have someone who was disabled heading their baseball league. No, the mayor wasn't in a wheelchair. No, there weren't many kids playing in their baseball league who had handicaps.

It was just time to stand up and be counted for what was right. Nick Sterio, a Palermo Youth Organization coach who operates a crane at the Alco Aluminum Co., was the first individual in the area to get upset by what happened to Tucker Church. He read an Associated Press wire story about Tucker in the *Syracuse Post-Standard*. He immediately reread it. And then he wept.

"I was trying," he said, "to determine if I was really reading the story right. I couldn't figure out why Little League was acting that way toward a handicapped kid. It just seemed mean to me. It didn't seem right. You know, I felt really bad for the adults that did that to Tucker, too. They were so far gone they didn't realize what they could do to a kid. That's such a shame."

You hear that repeatedly as you talk to people in Palermo. "It just didn't seem right to us, that's why we did what we did," said Patty Redhead, who was the president of the Palermo Youth Organization in 1989.

"It didn't seem right to anybody in town," Savage said.

Sterio called a reporter at the Syracuse paper to see if he could give him any leads on how he could reach the Church family. The newsman informed him that the story originated in the *Houston Post*.

He called the *Post* and asked me for the Churches' phone number.

I told him that I was sure the Church family would be touched by a call. I learned from Sterio that he was "just a blue-collar guy" that doesn't like to see kids get hurt. He had played Little League ball himself, he said, and liked the Palermo Youth Organization's approach better.

"There's not all the cut-throat stuff and we do everything we can to accommodate handicapped kids and everybody else," he said. "You know, the more I talk about this, the more upset I get."

After I gave Sterio the phone number for the Churches, I doubted that his interest would go any further than expressing his sympathy. That was a nice gesture, but nothing really to write about.

The next day I received a call from Judi Church. She seemed stunned. Nick Sterio had told her that everyone in the Palermo Youth Organization was going to wear a yellow armband as a show of support. He also said he'd be getting back in contact with her later.

"Can you believe complete strangers doing this sort of thing?" Judi said.

It wasn't long before Sterio and Redhead started a fundraising effort to bring Tucker and his family and his coach to Palermo. They decided that what had happened to Tucker Church symbolized to them everything baseball for kids shouldn't be, everything they had tried to make sure that the Palermo Youth Organization wasn't. This would be their way of making a statement. This would show the children of Palermo that you have to stand up for what's right.

Why should adults be allowed to ruin the joy of children? Why should adults make things any tougher for a child with cerebral palsy?

Everyone, it seemed—in a community where the median income is around thirty thousand dollars—pitched in some money. One youngster gave Sterio every one of his four pennies. There was a country-western jamboree fund-raiser. Businesses, firemen, cops, farmers—they all gave. In less than a week there was enough money— sixteen hundred dollars—to bring Tucker and his mother and dad and younger brother Josh to Palermo. And Tucker's coach, Scott Davis, too.

It was the first and only time that the city of Palermo had ever done such a thing.

"I'm so proud that everybody realized that what had been done was wrong and wanted to stand up and say so," Sterio said.

When Redhead and Sterio let Judi Church know about

what the town wanted to do, she couldn't speak. She choked back tears. At first, the people in Palermo thought there was a bad connection or that she had hung up. Finally, she said, "I don't know what to say."

Tucker, who also talked with Sterio on the phone, immediately found a soul mate in the father of two. Sterio had told him that the most important thing to him was people being fair and decent with each other. That's all Tucker wanted people to be. "We'd really be honored if you came, Tucker," the thirty-five-year-old Sterio said. "All the kids want to meet the guy who was in the newspaper."

Tucker threw his fist in the air. He was going to Palermo! He decided he'd better look at a map to find out where it was.

The group from Houston arrived at the Syracuse airport on July 7, 1989. Banners and posters emblazoned with "Welcome Tucker and Family" decorated the airport as more than two hundred well-wishers applauded their arrival. Tucker was already wearing the "PYO" baseball cap and jersey that had been sent to him. There was a limo to take them to Palermo, the same limo that had squired rock star Bruce Springsteen around when he played the Carrier Dome at Syracuse University. "Oh, man, a limo," Tucker said as he sank down in the soft leather interior of the stretch Cadillac.

Tucker tried to watch the countryside but he found himself closing his eyes a lot on the drive, too. He thought about what had happened in the last few weeks. Interviews, throwing out the first pitch at the Astrodome, meeting all the big leaguers, playing in his last game—the images flooded through his mind and actually made him dizzy. It had all happened so fast. Then he said something to no one in particular. "There really are a lot of nice people around." For awhile no one said anything. Then Judi Church got a tissue to wipe her eyes. Coach Scott

Davis, a broad smile on his face, couldn't resist drawling: "I just never thought I'd see the day when New Yorkers did something like this for Texans."

It was time to party.

First, there was a barbecue to go to at Patty and Bill Redhead's place. The arrivals were met with applause there, too. Terry Church introduced his wife, their eight-year-old son, Josh, and Davis and Tucker.

"We're family now," Judi said as she relaxed around a picnic table with Sterio and other new friends. Tucker held court with the youngsters from the Palermo league, telling them what it was like to throw out the first pitch at a big league ballgame and to meet the major leaguers out on the Astrodome playing field. Several youngsters asked Tucker to autograph baseballs. They had never met anyone so famous before. Later, they all played badminton.

"It was a side of America people don't hear about too much—the good side," Judi said. "We need to tell people about it more when we see it and experience it."

The Churches stayed at the home of Bill and Nancy Kilin for the four days they were in Palermo.

"They made us feel just like family," Terry Church said. "It's really something that strangers would do something like this."

They went to an air show and to a minor league ballgame between the Syracuse Chiefs and Rochester Redwings. The five thousand people on hand gave Tucker a standing ovation as it was announced he would throw out the first pitch. Fans from all over the stands came to get autographs from him.

"That really got to me," Tucker said. "It was like people wanted to be around someone who had put up a fight against Little League. One man said he had pulled his kid out of Little League because the adults were so rule-crazy."

Two days after he arrived—on a crisp Sunday morning—Tucker learned that the Oswego County Legislature and the Palermo Town Board had officially declared the day Tucker Church Day. Government officials said the people of Palermo wanted Tucker Church Day to serve as a symbol for all handicapped kids in America who want a chance to grow and play like other children. On his day, Tucker got to play an inning with each of the four teams in a special game set up by the Palermo Youth Organization. When he hit a home run, he spotted Nick Sterio as he was rounding third and ran into his arms.

"That meant an awful lot to me," Sterio said. "Actually, people kept focusing on how much this all meant to Tucker, but it meant an awful lot to us, too. Do you realize that our kids hadn't been around someone with cerebral palsy before? Now they know that people with that condition are just regular people who have more difficulty getting around."

And you can bet those Palermo kids, just in the course of their everyday lives, will spread the message around. One by one, person by person, that's how bigotry is broken down. That's why mainstreaming of the disabled is so crucial in American society.

Tucker received The Most Valuable Player trophy from the youth organization and Scott Davis was named Coach of the Year. Eddie Cook was one of the youngsters who stood in line to pump Tucker's hand and get his picture taken with him.

"I don't understand," Eddie said, "how Little League could go after such a nice guy."

As Patty Redhead watched Tucker play with the Palermo kids, she became more convinced than ever that the twelve-year-old Palermo Youth Organization was on the right track. Money was hardly a factor, with the ten-dollar registration fee waived if a child's family couldn't afford it. And kids play with kids according to their ability. Age isn't the big determining factor. Everyone gets a trophy at the end the season.

"If you have true local control, it's very easy to bend the rules for the good of a youngster," she said. "Once we even had a runner who would run with a deaf child. Nobody cared. It was just the way it was. If somebody's in a wheelchair and can swing the bat, he can play. That's it. No big deal."

Sterio and the Church family became so close that five

weeks later, the coach from Palermo visited the Churches at their Houston home. Tucker frequently talks with Sterio on the phone, always reminding him of the time in New York when Sterio took him to a movie, tripped over his own feet, and fell to the floor. "Remember, I'm supposed to be the guy who has trouble getting around," Tucker says.

Tucker didn't want to leave Palermo. It isn't often that you're treated like a hero. The Palermo children didn't want him to leave either. They had all learned a lot.

"What the kids really learned," Patty Redhead said, "is that you stand up for what you think is right and fight for it. I think it's a heckuva message to learn at any age."

Who can argue with that?

Judi Church says she learned once and for all that Tucker had a bright future ahead of him. She saw his confidence "zoom off the charts" in Palermo. "Even if nothing else had happened to him, he was going to be okay, I knew that."

The fact that the people of Palermo were just regular people who did what they did impressed him immensely. They were making a stand and he understood that. After all, that's what he felt like by not playing until Scott coached. And these people genuinely liked him, really laughed at his jokes. They particularly loved two of them:

"Did you hear about the New Yorker who willed his body to science? Science is contesting the will."

"There was a feud between two Texas neighbors. One refused to let the other take a shortcut through his property. Now the man has to go eight hundred miles out of his way to get home."

As he went around Palermo, Tucker found himself repeating, "There really are a lot of nice people around."

Nick Sterio hoped Palermo had sent a message to Little League headquarters.

"I wanted them to be interested in something more than collecting their fees. I wanted them to know that the American people don't want handicapped people treated badly, that the American people are better than that."

Little League Baseball Inc. didn't get the message.

Chapter 12

If you still wonder if what happened to Tucker Church in Little League was an aberration—an example of insensitivity toward the disabled far removed from the everyday mind-set of the organization's top brass—the treatment of Larry Anderson and Julie Henry should prove telling.

In spite of the passage of the Americans with Disabilities Act, signed into law by President Bush in 1990, much discrimination still exists. For three years, Julie Henry, a thirteen-year-old seventh grader with severe hearing problems, wore a special batting helmet with only one complete protective flap during her Little League softball games in Pennsylvania. A right-handed batter, her left ear, the one facing the pitcher, was fully protected by the helmet. Her right ear was not.

Her doctor, Dr. James M. Chicklo, of Chambersburg, Pennsylvania, explained why the special helmet was needed:

"For Julie to wear a helmet with a flap [over the right ear] would not be advisable... One reason being the flap would cause feedback from the [hearing] aid which could cause further damage to her hearing. Secondly, with the flap she would have to turn the hearing aid down so low as not to cause feedback which would render the hearing aid useless to her...A softball most likely still wouldn't get through the cut-out area to harm the ear."

Little League officials said that a one-flap helmet couldn't be safe, even though they let Julie play first base, where she's repeatedly thrown the ball in a cloth cap. The officials were adamant: They didn't care what Julie's doctor said. Or that the family was willing to sign any liability waiver Little League would give them. When they found out Julie wasn't wearing the Little League's specified helmet, they gave her an ultimatum: to wear the helmet or stop playing. The U.S. Justice Department is investigating Little League's behavior.

"I just can't believe how ugly Little League is toward people who have some kind of disability," said Anderson, a wheelchair-bound Little League coach who also happens to be a superior court judge in Phoenix, Arizona.

Could Little League official Creighton Hale really have thought that Anderson would resign himself to a new Little League rule against coaches in wheelchairs when he had coached at first and third base for three years without incident? Did Hale think Anderson would say, Okay, I give up, when he courageously came back from a terrible car accident? Did Hale think Anderson wouldn't fight when he had the support of everyone in the league, including a former major league baseball star and the team orthopedist for the National Football League's Phoenix Cardinals?

Anderson was a man so highly thought of that he was selected to coach the All Star Games in Phoenix, Arizona, in 1991 and 1992. And this was also a man who knew everything about the Americans with Disabilities Act (ADA), which was enacted by the U.S. Congress on July 26, 1990.

Anderson (whose eleven-year-old son Luke plays on his team) grew up in Arizona, where his father practiced law. After the car accident that left Anderson in a wheelchair, he fought through both the physical pain and emotional heartache to graduate from the University of San Francisco. He later attended law school at Arizona State University.

It was during the summer of 1991 that National Little

League officials learned that Anderson was coaching in a wheelchair. They acted swiftly.

A July 24, 1991, memorandum from Carlton Magee, the western region director, to Mike Kayes, the district administrator for Anderson's league, explains why:

"Little League must consider the safety of the youth playing the game, and they should not have the added concern of avoiding a collision with a wheelchair during their participation in the game."

Kayes was incensed. He fired off a letter to Magee on July 25, 1991:

"...It is my opinion that this alleged policy reflects negatively upon the organization for which I volunteer. It makes no sense and has the aroma of discrimination thinly veiled under the guise of legitimate concerns. In short, I find the policy repulsive and I believe it to be a moral, ethical and legal affront to courageous individuals who are (and should be) protected both by law and public policy from precisely this sort of covert discrimination.

"I fully intend to disregard this policy and provide fair and equal opportunities for all managers, coaches and players. For me to do less would compromise both my humanity and morality, neither of which are within the control of Little League Baseball..."

The local Little League did, in fact, refuse to enforce the national policy. A major showdown over the rule didn't occur in 1991, however, because Anderson's team was knocked out of tournament play.

During the off-season, the state district administrators of the Little League voted as an organization to oppose the policy and seek its reversal.

Dennis H. Miller, the president of Miller/Russell & Associates, Inc., in Arizona, tried to get Hale to see the light in a January 13, 1992, letter:

Dr. Creighton Hale:

Last year I managed a major league team within

Arcadia Little League, Phoenix, Arizona (District
6). By virtue of the fact that my team placed second
in league play I had the added pleasure of being
named coach of our all-star team, and as such
assisted a Mr. Larry Anderson throughout the
practice sessions and tournament play. Larry was
named manager of the team by the board of
directors, which is a "right of passage" extended
to the manager of the team placing first in league
play. In addition to guiding his team to first place,
Larry is also a fine person who exhibits all of the
traits the board of directors seeks when selecting
an all-star manager. He is a fine example for young
people.

Mr. Anderson is unique to most coaches since
he is confined to a wheelchair. However, his
disability goes relatively unnoticed in our league
because he does not allow it to stand in the way.
You should know that Larry is a former wheelchair
weight lifting champion, has played wheelchair
basketball, developed a successful law practice and
presently serves as a judge in criminal court.

In regular league play Larry was often on the
field in game situations. However, an umpire filed
a protest against his on-field activity (third-base
coach) during the all-star tournament because he
was an "unsafe obstacle," and wanted him confined
to the dugout. As I understand, the District 6
President would not support the umpire's
complaint, and she subsequently moved the action
to either California or your office, where it was in
fact determined that a person in a wheelchair is at
higher risk to himself and players than can be
accepted by Little League Baseball Inc., and
consequently Larry would indeed be restricted to
the dugout. I presume this decision related to a
specific rule or set of rules. We lost our next game
and exited from the tournament before this final
ruling came forth, but virtually everyone involved,

including the District 6 office, now feels very uncomfortable with the ruling and the precedent that it sets for others with a disability.

...[Anderson is] an excellent coach and role model for young people, many who are in the process of forming what will be life-long opinions about those who have disabilities. It is impossible to read the creed of Little League and think about our changing world, without feeling a gross injustice is taking place.

Now this entire incident is meaningful to me not simply because of my respect for Larry Anderson, but in a larger sense due to my concern about many others with disabilities who may also be restricted from normal activities by Little League Baseball. For nearly fifteen years I have served in various capacities with the Easter Seal Society and presently serve as a national board member... Through this period of time I have seen great changes in our national attitudes toward disabled people, and feel society is enhanced by such change, accordingly I champion the elimination of all discriminatory practices that are barriers to participation.

Correspondingly, those who have a disability are participating more actively in all walks of life, and can come to see themselves as only "inconvenienced," not disadvantaged. If we all pull together, and welcome participation regardless of how awkward it may sometimes be seen, it is possible to eliminate the "dis" from disability. I recognize that to allow full or appropriate levels of participation in business or personal activity may sometimes be costly or add risk, but isn't life full of trade-offs?

...I feel that the decision rendered by Little League Baseball with respect to Larry Anderson's on-field activity was unfair and needs review, and I further suspect that on a larger scale rules regarding people with disabilities may be discriminatory throughout the organization. And, they certainly may not be in compliance with the Americans With Disabilities Act recently enacted by Congress, which as you know carries significant penalties for law violations.

At this point I need to have a better understanding of Little League Baseball rules regarding on-field safety and how that subject relates to players or coaches with a disability. What constitutes an "unsafe condition"? What provisions can be made to encourage participation from a disabled person? Are we flexible? Why can't district officers participate in deciding such issues? What is the policy regarding disabilities, etc.? So, I would greatly appreciate opening a dialogue with you or a staff member over my concerns and questions. This is not an issue which I will let die easily and would hope to have resolved before the forthcoming baseball season...

Sincerely,
Dennis H. Miller

Hale wrote Miller back on January 24, 1992.

"...This issue has been carefully studied and it is the position of the [rules] committee that the logic of the ruling was for the purpose of minimizing unnecessary hazards to the young players.

"It has been brought to our attention that similar rulings have been made relative to the use of crutches by individuals in the coaching box and certainly an individual in a wheelchair would have more difficulty in avoiding sudden traffic than a crutch-user..."

Say what? Anybody who's used both crutches and a wheelchair would beg to differ. A wheelchair athlete like Anderson, a former college baseball player who has become a weight-lifting champion, can move faster than many, many people with two good legs.

In March 1992, David Capozzi, vice president of the National Easter Seal Society, wrote Hale, trying to get him to see the futility and ugliness of his position.

Dear Dr. Hale:

...On January 13, 1992 , Mr. Dennis Miller wrote to you about...Mr. Larry Anderson...and you responded..."that the logic of the ruling was for the purpose of minimizing unnecessary hazards to the young players." Your letter went on to compare the abilities of people who use crutches to those who use wheelchairs. You indicated that "similar rulings have been made relative to the use of crutches by individuals in the coaching box and certainly an individual in a wheelchair would have more difficulty... I believe that you may not have considered the individual facts in this case and did not examine the capabilities of Mr. Anderson specifically to coach Little League baseball safely.

Also, at least two significant events have occurred since you made your initial decision. The public accommodations provisions of the Americans with Disabilities Act are now effective and a ruling was recently issued by the Indiana Civil Rights Commission on a similar issue... In my opinion, by preventing Mr. Anderson from coaching, he is being discriminated against because of his disability by Little League Baseball, Inc.

Last month the Indiana Civil Rights Commission ruled that a female high school softball coach who uses a three-wheeled, battery-powered mobility device must be allowed to coach on the field in her motorized cart. The woman, Sandra Childers, is a paraplegic and coached first base at Sheridan High School in Hamilton County.

Based on these developments, I request that you reconsider your decision to prohibit Mr. Anderson from participating in on-field Little League coaching activities. Mr. Anderson is a fine role model for children and it would be a shame if someone with his talents and desire to volunteer his time is precluded from making a contribution to the game of baseball and the lives of impressionable children...

Sincerely,
David Capozzi

Capozzi's well-thought out plea was ignored. In June 1992, the Little League rules committee that Hale serves on affirmed its earlier decision. Coaches in wheelchairs couldn't go in the coach's box.

It didn't matter to the Little League brass that Americans had said overwhelmingly in the Tucker Church affair that they didn't want things made difficult for the disabled when an accommodation could easily be made. It didn't matter that the entire town of Palermo, New York, had taken a stand against Little League's treatment of the handicapped. It didn't matter that every Little League official in Arizona, save one coach, believed that Anderson should be allowed to manage from the third-base line. It didn't matter that all the kids thought he should be able to coach. It didn't matter that the Americans with Disabilities Act seemed clear about how to handle such a situation. No, what mattered to the Little League brass was that the risk of a kid running into Anderson's wheelchair was too great!

On July 3, 1992, Creighton Hale sent a letter to presidents of all Arizona Little Leagues, warning them that they would all run the risk of being thrown out of Little League if they allowed a handicapped person to coach:

"This is to advise you we have been made aware of certain local agreements...which if pursued would violate conditions of charter and tournament participation. This could and would result in disqualifying the league from tournament play and loss of the charter for a violation of a Little League Board of Director's Policy pertaining to qualifying persons occupying the coach's boxes."

On July 6, 1992, Anderson, who wanted to see Little

League's money spent on kids, not lawyers, did what he had never wanted to do. He filed suit against Little League Baseball and Creighton Hale, asking a federal court for a restraining order that would prevent the organization from keeping him off the field.

Chris Speier, who played professional baseball for twenty years with the San Francisco Giants, Montreal Expos, Chicago Cubs, and Minnesota Twins, couldn't believe what was going on. He had been involved in an Arizona Little League program and had observed Anderson both on and off the field. His own children played on teams that played against Anderson's.

In an affidavit he wrote: "Based on my experiences as a professional baseball player, as well as my exposure to Coach Anderson, I do not believe that Coach Anderson's presence on the field during play poses any threat to the health or safety of players, umpires, or other participants."

Dr. Russell Chick, who worked with the Los Angeles Dodgers prior to becoming the team orthopedist for the Phoenix Cardinals, noted in his affidavit that his son played both for and against Coach Anderson.

He said that as a licensed medical doctor, and from what he had seen of Coach Anderson's work on the baseball field, "I don't believe that Coach Anderson's presence on the field during play poses any threat to the health or safety of players, umpires, or other participants."

It was time to go to court, to spend more Little League money in the courtroom.

U.S. District Court Judge Earl H. Carroll didn't take long to make a decision. On July 8 he handed down a temporary restraining order against Little League. His discussion of the Americans With Disabilities Act is invaluable, arguably the most concise and most understandable treatment of the massive civil rights legislation yet provided. He wrote in part:

"...The Americans with Disabilities Act" was enacted on July 26, 1990. In passing the Act, Congress recognized that one or more physical or mental disabilities affect

more than forty-three million Americans whom society
has tended to isolate and segregate because of their
disabilities.

"The Act's Subchapter III—Public Accommodations and
Services Operated by Private Entities, which became
effective on January 26, 1992, provides as follows: 'No
individual shall be discriminated against on the basis of
disability in the full and equal enjoyment of the goods,
services, facilities, privileges, advantages, or
accommodation by any person who owns, leases (or leases
to), or operates a place of public accommodation.'

"Many disabled people lead isolated lives and do not
frequent places of public accommodation. The extent of
non-participation of individuals with disabilities in social
and recreational activities is alarming. The United States
Attorney General has stated that we must bring Americans
with disabilities into the mainstream of society, in other
words, full participation in and access to all aspects of
society...

"...There is no indication... that defendants (Little
League and Hale) conducted an individualized assessment
and determined that plaintiff (Anderson) poses a direct
threat to the health and safety of others... Regrettably,
such a policy—implemented without public discourse—
falls markedly short of the requirements enunciated in
the Americans with Disabilities Act and its implementing
regulations."

In effect, then, National Little League officials—who
guide a program that is supposedly a moral beacon for
youngsters—had done nothing more than engage in the
most primitive kind of prejudice under the guise of safety
concerns. Under Hale's leadership, no attempt was even
made to show that Anderson was a threat to anyone. Just
the thought of him in a wheelchair by the third-base line
meant that National Little League officials felt compelled
to discriminate.

Judge Carroll summed up his order eloquently:

The court gives great weight to the fact that plaintiff (Anderson) has served as a Little League coach at either first base or third base for three years without incident. Moreover, plaintiff's significant contributions of time, energy and enthusiasm and personal example benefit the numerous children who participate in Little League activities as well as the community at large. Plaintiff's work with young people teaches them the importance of the strengths of others and helping them rise to overcome their personal challenges.

The court has no doubt that both plaintiff and the children with whom he works will suffer irreparable harm if defendants are permitted to arguably discriminate against plaintiff based on his disability. Such discrimination is clearly contrary to public policy and the interests of society as a whole. In particular, such discrimination is contrary to the interests of plaintiff and everyone who is interested or participates in Little League activities, including the defendant organization (Little League) and its officers (Hale etc.).

After the ruling was handed down, Anderson talked with *USA Today* about the effect the case had had on him. The story about his battle appeared on the front page of the national newspaper's sports section. "My emotions have been up and down," he said. "I haven't had much sleep."

As he sat in a restaurant following the ruling, a steady stream of people walked up to congratulate him on his victory. He told the well-wishers that he hoped his case would have a great effect on future cases.

"I've had numerous parents from all over the country calling me," Anderson said, including Jill Henry, the mother of hearing-impaired Julie Henry. He noted that Little League was using the same tactics on Julie for wearing a special helmet as it did with him, threatening to remove all teams from official Little League competition if she was allowed to play.

Anderson made it clear he despised the threatening

tactic that had also been used in the Tucker Church affair. "It didn't work, and I wasn't going to take these bullying tactics," he said. "I tried for a year to resolve this without litigation, trying to keep in mind what's best for the kids."

With Tucker Church winning his case in the court of public opinion and Anderson winning his at the federal courthouse and with both cases getting such heavy national media attention, you would think Little League officials would get the message the American people were clearly sending: Stop trying to cripple the disabled!

They haven't.

And that is of particular concern to Judge Anderson.

"I'm worried that there are many people out there who don't have the time or the resources to fight Little League," he said. "They end up being hurt real bad, accepting the discrimination. Many people who are disabled don't like being in the public eye, so they don't go to the media."

Julie Henry and her family are definitely fighting for what they think is right. Like the Church family, they have been presented with more than their share of challenges. But after overcoming so much hardship and tragedy, they find it unthinkable that they would let narrow-minded Little League officials get the best of them.

"To accept discrimination after what we've been through would be like finally giving up on life," said Jill Henry, Julie's mother.

In 1981, Jill Henry was diagnosed with Crohn's Disease, and she spent seven years in and out of hospitals before developing other immunity problems. In April 1983, Julie's father, Barry, fell from a crane he was working on and suffered a broken neck, a broken shoulder, and a severely lacerated face. He was laid up for fourteen months. Then, just after Barry Henry returned to work, the Henrys' oldest son, Jamie, was struck by a car and killed instantly. There was hardly time to grieve because, two days after Jamie's death, a doctor diagnosed Julie with a rapid hearing loss from an unknown cause. Not until five months later was it determined that a perilymphatic fistula of the brain had leaked into both of her inner ears. She has undergone eleven surgeries and can now hear in one ear with the help of a high-powered hearing aid.

Mainstreamed in school, Julie is an excellent student. She also became an all-star Little League softball player. But then in the spring of 1992 national officials found out about the special one-flap batting helmet she wore because of the hearing aid in her right ear. The threat was made—either she would wear a two-flap helmet or all the teams in her league would be kicked out of Little League.

Julie began to wear a helmet with two flaps, one that was extra large so that it would not put pressure on her hearing aid.

In a letter to Colleen Miller, the attorney with the U.S. Department of Justice that is now investigating Little League's behavior, Jill Henry outlined what happened:

> Ms. Miller:
> First, Julie wore the helmet with the [hearing] aid turned down. There was no feedback while she was standing still and had the large helmet on. The helmet was so large that she had to wear a strap on it to keep it from falling off. She placed the helmet tight against the left ear so there was enough space at her right ear so the hearing aid wouldn't feed back. She still couldn't hear that well. The minute Julie would try to swing at the ball or run, her aid would feed back. She called many timeouts. There are only so many timeouts in a game you can call before umps, coaches, and teammates get frustrated and start making comments. Because of having the feedbacks and possibility of losing the eardrum that she has, she played deaf. When you are in fear that a ball will hit you, how can you concentrate on a game?

She also could not hear balls and strikes, and how are you to lip read when you have your back to the ump? At one game, she didn't hear the ump tell her that there was a bat on the field. It was an embarrassing moment for Julie when everyone was screaming at her to get the bat off the field and looking up to realize everyone has been screaming at her...

...Granted, if Julie being deaf, had chosen to play softball, she would just have to adjust to these conditions. However, she is not totally deaf. If she were, she wouldn't hear the cruel comments. This situation has put a great strain on my daughter, both emotionally and physically... Emotionally, I have seen Julie go through the initial grieving process all over again that people go through when they lose a part of themselves to a disability. As parents, it's been very heartbreaking when we know it's not necessary... Even though she can communicate with both worlds, she was born a hearing child and prefers the hearing world. Our thinking about this softball situation is, why should we lower Julie's standard of life?"

Sincerely,
Barry and Jill Henry

Because the Justice Department is conducting an investigation, Colleen Miller said she could not comment on the case. Jill Henry did say in February 1993, that pressure from the U.S. Department of Justice had forced Little League to make her an offer: Julie could play Little League ball as long as she waived all liability rights.

That doesn't seem fair to the Henrys. If Julie were to get hurt during an incident on the playing field that had nothing to do with her hearing, then she wouldn't be covered by insurance. In mid-February of 1993, the Henrys and Little League officials were still trying to work out a compromise.

National Little League officials have encouraged Julie, as they did with Judge Anderson and Tucker, to join the

Challenger division of Little League, a program for the severely disabled.

"Why should we do that when we're able to compete in the world?" Judge Anderson asked. "All they're trying to do is get us out of the way. It's their way of warehousing people. It's time for some more enlightened minds at the head of Little League. Our country has said, through legislation and even much change in attitude, that the way to deal with the disabled is 'not out of sight, out of mind.'"

Julie Henry can't hide her disappointment.

"I've been with normal people all my life," she said. "And now they're trying to separate me when there's no need to. Everything went great for three years. Basically, they just think I'm a bother."

Julie's happy she has her parents' support.

"A parent has to fight for their kids," she said. "Because otherwise, you're just going to get stepped on."

Tucker Church now realizes he was naive.

"I had thought my situation might stop Little League and everybody else from acting mean toward people who were a little different," he said.

That hasn't been the case for Pam Mackie.

Pam Mackie made a mistake five years ago, and she's paid for it dearly.

She can't run anymore.

She can't walk anymore.

She can't play the guitar anymore.

She can't work on cars anymore.

She can't type fast enough to be a secretary anymore.

So it sometimes happens when you make a mistake on a motorcycle.

She shouldn't have looked back to see if her friends were coming while she was riding a Harley Davidson. If she hadn't, she would have seen that the road made a Y, and that if she went straight she'd hit a sign welcoming people to a Houston neighborhood.

But the five-foot-eight redhead did look over her shoulder. And she hit the sign, flew through the air, and landed at the base of a tree.

She ended up a quadriplegic in a wheelchair.

There was a time when the twenty-nine-year-old spent a good part of every day focusing on what she couldn't do. That caused her to plan her suicide. Then a friend got her to make a deal: if after a year she still didn't think she could have a life with purpose, she could go ahead and kill herself.

It didn't take a year for Pam to realize she could still contribute. She took courses in computer programming and she's closing in on a college degree in psychology.

What has been more difficult than choosing life over death, she says, is the realization that society isn't all that keen on accommodating her desire to be a contributor, a builder, a worker on behalf of humanity.

She can't understand why the kind of public concern shown for Tucker Church in his battle with Little League doesn't transfer to all disabled.

She's not jealous, or envious.

She just doesn't understand.

"It seems kind of crazy," she says, "that people can't see that what's wrong for one person is wrong for another."

Disabled men and women followed the Tucker Church affair closely. So did parents of children with disabilities. The public outcry appeared to show that sentiment was behind accommodating them. It seemed as though the public had realized that fair play was in order.

But even before the Tucker Church story really died down, Peggy Smith was barred from boarding the cruise-gaming ship, Pride of Mississippi, because a ship official said the wheelchair-bound woman's presence would make other passengers "uncomfortable."

That sad affair played out in Galveston, Texas, considered part of the Greater Houston area. Bowing to public pressure, the ship's owners decided later to let the disabled come aboard.

"Why does everything have to be a fight?" asked one young man in a wheelchair. "What was the whole Tucker Church thing about?"

Dr. Ken Krajewski, who ended up in a wheelchair after being struck by a polio-like virus in his youth, found he couldn't take his five-year-old son on an excursion train between Houston and Galveston. The man who had quietly gone along proving that people should be liberated by their abilities rather than imprisoned by their disabilities, was outraged.

He, too, wanted to know why the same kinds of battles had to be fought again and again.

"America stands for human rights," he said. "They're our strongest arsenals. They're a major reason that people in communist countries have brought down their governments: They haven't had human rights. Our society could perish the same way. We should see discrimination of any kind as an act of treason."

Believe it or not, Pam Mackie, who was so encouraged by the public's response to Tucker's troubles, had to struggle to even become part of the Big Brothers and Big Sisters of Houston. And this is an organization that sets itself up as caring, compassionate, humanistic. When she called the headquarters of the organization, she was told that the organization didn't accept disabled youngsters, so there was no need for her as a Big Sister.

After the media called the organization's headquarters, the message changed and she was able to undergo training to become a Big Sister.

"Nobody gets the whole message that should have been learned from Tucker Church's experience and so many others that get publicized," Pam said. "We go over the same ground all the time."

Chapter 13

Lex Frieden, one of the most effective civil rights activists in American history, sits at a table in the outdoor dining area of The Institute for Rehabilitation and Research (TIRR) in Houston and talks about attitudes toward the disabled.

We have met for lunch and the chief architect of the Americans with Disabilities Act (ADA) lets his enchiladas get cold. It is quickly apparent that the forty-three-year-old Frieden appreciates food for thought far more than food for the belly. He is a trim man, sitting in a wheelchair as a result of an auto accident during his freshman year of college. A senior vice president of TIRR who worked in Washington, D.C., for years conceiving the ADA legislation, he was awarded the Presidential Citation by George Bush for his distinguished Service to America in promoting the dignity, equality, independence, and employment of people with disabilities.

For a man whose work will radically change America—the effects of ADA are only now beginning to be felt across the country—Frieden is remarkably modest. He tries to stay out of the limelight, worried that media attention on a personality rather than on the work ahead might weaken the effectiveness of the civil rights movement. "The drive for what has been done and what needs to be done comes from millions of people," he says. "That isn't something we can lose."

He, too, has followed the Tucker Church story. He is not happy that Tucker's highly-publicized battle didn't change the behavior of more people, but he's not surprised that it didn't. "Unfortunately," he says, "nothing comes all that easily for people with disabilities." He's the kind of man who takes a historical perspective, who can tell you that in the ancient Hebrew culture, where illness and physical impairments were associated with sin, the social stigma attached to such conditions was quite strong. He'll also tell you that the relationship between attitudes and behavior was clearly evident in the militaristic society of ancient Sparta, where all malformed babies were thrown off a precipice.

Frieden is a close friend of Frank Bowe, who wrote *Handicapping America.*

Positive changes for those with disabilities in America, Bowe wrote, have come in fits and starts. The earliest colonists restricted immigration by those with disabilities because they might need financial support. Rarely did anyone think that someone with a disability could achieve financial self-sufficiency. And the idea of rehabilitation and education so someone could overcome a disability seldom, if ever, came up. Children and adults with disabilities were cared for by families, and often hidden away.

It wasn't until late in the seventeenth century that almshouses came into being to provide food and shelter for poor and disabled individuals. And it wasn't until the middle of the eighteenth century that educational and medical services became available. Mental hospitals and schools for the deaf and blind were created.

When disabled people were allowed to work, they seldom left the institutions, which were most notable for their appalling, unsanitary conditions. People didn't want to be offended by the sight of men and women with disabilities. A significant change for the better occurred after servicemen with disabilities resulting from World War I returned from the war and suffered severe adjustment problems. The Smith-Sears Vocational Rehabilitation Act, which funded job training and education for disabled veterans, was passed in 1918. Institutionalization, Americans were saying, wasn't the only way to go.

During the war, large numbers of disabled individuals had demonstrated their ability to work when they took jobs left open by those who left to fight. So impressed was Congress that in 1920, members passed the Vocational Rehabilitation Act for civilians who were disabled.

It was the election of Franklin Roosevelt to the Presidency in 1932, however, that provoked a major change in America's treatment of the disabled. Though his legs had been paralyzed by polio, he was a confident, can-do individual who led the country toward prosperity. Soon after he took office, he signed the Social Security Act that established programs for disabled children and adults as well as old-age and survivors' benefits, and unemployment compensation. Assistance to disabled people had become an act of social justice instead of charity. Roosevelt was also the impetus for legislation that enlarged vocational rehabilitation programs.

In the 1960s, the social turbulence provoked by the demands for equal opportunities for black Americans also spawned programs for disabled individuals. Activist groups like the Paralyzed Veterans of America began to make their voices heard. In the 1970s, legislation that included the Rehabilitation Act of 1973 would provide the impetus for the historic Americans with Disabilities Act that Frieden had a large hand in getting signed into law in 1990.

Up until his involvement with the ADA, Frieden, who was valedictorian of his high school class, was best known for his pioneering work in the independent living movement for handicapped people in the United States. After his accident, he required help with hygiene and dressing, but he didn't want to live with his parents or in a nursing home. He came up with the idea of a dormitory style of living where all the people had disabilities of one sort or another, but still ran the house. It worked, and eventually led to people living even more independent lives. That experiment has spread across the nation.

Wanting even more privacy, Frieden decided to move out of the dormitory. He had met Mac Brodie, who had suffered a head wound in Vietnam. The two developed what he calls a "symbiotic relationship." Frieden, whose intellect and ability to speak off the cuff reminds you of newsman Ted Koppel, helped Brodie, who had problems with his cognitive abilities. And Brodie, who had excellent use of his hands, helped Frieden, who has little use of his hands. Today, Brodie lives with Frieden and his wife, Joyce, who was disabled by a neurological disease.

Frieden says the only way attitudes are ever going to change toward those with disabilities is through contact with the able-bodied.

"We have goals just like anybody else," he says. "Once people see that, the 'us and them' mentality disappears."

The "us and them mentality" that Frieden refers to can be illustrated through the media's treatment of him. For instance, in Houston where he lives, he's never called on by media people to offer his expertise on working in Washington, or on lobbying, as he did so effectively on the ADA. When he is contacted, it's only in his capacity as a spokesman for those with disabilities. When the media needs "civil rights leaders," they contact African-Americans, Hispanics, and Asian-Americans. And yet Frieden's one of the most important civil rights leaders living in the United States today. What he first wrote in the mid-eighties can now be found in the ADA.

In March 1993, Frieden delivered a speech to the First Ladies from the countries of the Western Hemisphere who gathered in Washington, D.C. In effect, he called on each nation to pass legislation that would allow their disabled citizens to make their own way in the world. "A sage philosopher once observed," Frieden said, "that the best way to measure a society is to examine the way in which it treats its people with disabilities. The nations of the Western Hemisphere can demonstrate to the world the quality and strength of their society by bringing people with disabilities into the mainstream through the systematic introduction of laws and policies which foster inclusion, independence, productivity, and equal opportunity for people with disabilities."

When he gets the chance, Frieden shares the story of

his life with youngsters and teenagers like Tucker who have disabilities. He hopes it gives *them* hope. It does.

It was November 20, 1967. Frieden was in his freshman year at Oklahoma State University when the driver of the car he was riding in tried to pass a long line of cars. A head-on collision left everybody with minor injuries except for Frieden. He had been in the back seat, and the pileup caused his head to slam into the closed roof of the Camaro convertible. His head whipped backward and his neck was broken. At first, he thought operations would take care of the problem. Broken bones would be set and then they'd heal. But three weeks later, he saw a movie with Marlon Brando which concerned a character who had been paralyzed in the Korean War. Doctors called the man a quadriplegic. Frieden asked the doctor if that was his diagnosis. The doctor wouldn't give him a direct answer, saying instead that he had to focus on the abilities he had. That's when Frieden knew he was a quadriplegic.

An Oklahoma hospital sent him to The Institute for Rehabilitation and Research in Houston for specialized treatment. He wanted to return to college life and applied for admission to Oral Roberts University in his hometown of Tulsa, Oklahoma. The straight-A student was refused admission solely because he was handicapped. "That's the first time," he says, "that I realized that I didn't have control of my life the way I did before."

He ended up at the University of Tulsa, where he received his bachelor's degree in psychology. While he was there, his father told him about a meeting being held by a group of people with disabilities. Frieden didn't want to go, didn't want to be part of a "disabled group." He thought that by doing so, he'd become one of "them," as though he was someone to be ashamed of. His dad forced him into the car and made him go. "I was never so angry," Frieden says. "My father was taking advantage of the fact that I couldn't stop him from making me go. If I hadn't been hurt, I would never have gone."

It turned out to be a good move for him. It was during

that meeting and subsequent ones that he came to the conclusion that society should include everyone. It propelled him into staging demonstrations so the Houston bus fleet would be made accessible to everyone. "I had come to realize that the tax money of those with disabilities was being used for making sidewalks, and buying buses, so I decided they should be accessible to everyone." He did his graduate work at the University of Houston, where he continued his advocacy activities.

As renowned as he has become in the civil rights arena, he still has to endure slights. There have been times when he's been sitting with a cup of water in his hand at the bus stop and someone has come by and put money in it. Often, people will talk to an able-bodied person he's with, instead of to him, assuming that he can't talk because he's in a wheelchair.

Nothing could be worse at this time for disabled people, Frieden says, than a movement to segregate. "We have come too far, worked too hard, to allow anyone to force those with disabilities to go off by themselves," he said.

Tucker Church and his family worry that Little League officials may have deliberately perverted the message spawned by his confrontation with them and are now actively promoting segregation of disabled youngsters.

While Jim Ferguson, the director of Little League's special Challenger Division for the disabled, credits Tucker for "opening people's eyes to the fact that there's a need for disabled children to play an organized sport," Tucker and his parents are wary of that kind of words. Particularly if Ferguson's not doing all he can to mainstream youngsters.

In an interview in late 1992, Ferguson said Tucker's well-publicized battle with Little League played a major role in spurring interest by the disabled in playing baseball. In fact, he said that in 1989—the year of Tucker's struggle—fewer than three hundred children signed up.

Within months of his fight, Ferguson said thousands had signed up for the division. Today, thirty thousand youngsters are in the Challenger Division. Ferguson doesn't give Tucker all the credit, of course, but he does say his influence was critical.

Segregating disabled youngsters, unless it's absolutely necessary, goes entirely against the grain of the Church family's thinking. Mainstreaming the disabled is what they believe in. That concept is at the very core of the Americans with Disabilities Act. While Ferguson says children with minor disabilities are encouraged to play with the able-bodied, Tucker, and particularly his mom, aren't so sure.

Julie Henry's wearing of a hearing aid certainly seems minor. As disabilities go, that would seem to be one of the easiest to accommodate. And yet Little League officials, including Ferguson, are pushing her to enter the Challenger Division. Julie's mother said Ferguson has talked to her on several occasions about getting her daughter into the Challenger Division. Here's a girl who's been mainstreamed successfully in school, recreational activities, clubs, and church, but Little League says she's too disabled to play softball. (And remember she played softball successfully for three years until Little League decided she shouldn't be able to play with a special helmet that a doctor said was perfectly safe.)

It was also suggested to wheel-chair bound Little League coach Larry Anderson that he switch to the Challenger Division. Again, Judge Anderson had coached successfully for years in Little League until it was decided his wheelchair was a safety hazard to Little Leaguers. Instead of trying to work the disabled into the mix, Little League appears to be doing just the opposite under the guise of a caring program.

In February 1993, the state of Connecticut opened an investigation to see whether the Milford, Connecticut, Little League was discriminating against disabled children. The investigation was prompted by a complaint filed with the state Office of Protection and Advocacy for Persons

with Disabilities by an unnamed person, said Lawrence
Berliner, a lawyer for the agency. The complaint alleges
that the local Little League has policies that are
discriminatory because disabled children are not allowed
to play against children without disabilities.

Milford has a separate Challenger Division for children
with disabilities. Ron Funaro, president of the Milford
Little League, defended the policies of his program. He
said every child is given the opportunity to try out for a
team in any division. "If a kid is a good player and wants
to play outside the Challenger Division, then that kid
can," Funaro said.

It is critical to note that every researcher of any renown,
including Harold Yuker, Robert Kleck, and Jerome Siller,
has said that mainstreaming is the key both to alleviating
discrimination against the handicapped and to America
realizing the full potential of its citizenry.

You sense just how strongly Little League officials feel
about segregating the disabled when you read a
memorandum that National Little League official Joe Losch
wrote to Texas Little League director Mike Witherwax. It
was written after the Little League brass had bowed to
public pressure and said they would approve an age waiver
if Tucker got doctors' notes.

"The Committee," Losch wrote, "has approved Tucker
to participate in the Sharpstown minor league program
for the 1989 season only. Perhaps the parents may wish
to consider the Challenger program in 1990 as an
alternative for Tucker."

Incredible! After doctors, coaches, and players said
Tucker was both safe and competitive in actual games,
and he had played happily for eight years, Little League
was suggesting that he should enter a league where most
of the participants' disabilities were so severe that they
couldn't really offer Tucker any real competition.

"I can't help but wonder," Coach/Judge Anderson said,
"just how many youngsters Little League has placed in
the Challenger program when they should be in the
regular program."

The lessons drawn from baseball about competition and teamwork and sacrifice for a common cause are carried off the playing field. And let's face it: As competitive as American society is, we all need as many insights into how to compete successfully as possible. Chances of Tucker, for instance, getting a special "Challenger" job that he could raise a family on are slim to none. He needs to be able to compete with everyone. He, and as many disabled as possible, need to get into the mainstream. For their good, and ours.

Victoria Therrien is a mother who has found the Challenger Division a joyful experience for her fourteen-year-old son Nathan, who has Down's syndrome.

That is as it should be. If a child's disabilities are such that the Challenger Division is a challenge, it's a good opportunity. That league uses an "incrediball," which imitates a baseball but is made of softer stuff. All nine team members get to bat when their team is up. Contests are limited to four innings. There is generally no pitcher, although a player is assigned to field the mound area. Each player gets six swings at the ball and has the option of hitting off a tee or swinging at pitches thrown by a "buddy."

(A buddy is a volunteer, brother or sister, or fellow Little Leaguer who assists a player with a disability at bat or on the field. They push wheelchairs or run after balls a fielder can't get.)

"For years," Victoria Therrien wrote, "Nathan had participated in Special Olympics, and we tried to involve him in community sports. As he grew older and community sports became more competitive and skill-oriented, it was increasingly difficult to find a place for him... It was great knowing that Nathan wasn't going to be judged on his performance (in Challenger). Here he didn't have a label. He was praised for doing his best. He had achieved a new athletic milestone—becoming a baseball player. As the season ended for him, he had mixed emotions. He was disappointed that the program was ending; he wished it could go on all year. On the other hand he was happy. Playing baseball was "radical" to him. He felt proud when he received a trophy along with every other player in the Challenger Division..."

Those the Challenger Division really should provide a place for, then, are those who couldn't possibly compete in a regular Little League. Others should be mainstreamed.

"I was fortunate," Tucker says. "I was not disabled enough to where I couldn't compete at all. What I'm afraid Little League is trying to do is put everyone into Challenger even if they could play in a regular league, just to get those of us who aren't perfect out of the way."

America, through the Americans with Disabilities Act, has said that letting only children (and coaches) without "complications" be involved is a goal not worthy of a people who have come to realize that they must respect the frailties of man if they are going to move forward into a better world of their own making.

Chapter 14

Shriners have dedicated their organization to helping disabled children help themselves. They want to see physically disadvantaged youngsters become as whole as they can be. Nothing is more noble.

How their work is accomplished can be seen through Tucker Church.

In March 1990, Tucker was waiting in the doctor's office where his mother worked as a receptionist. A Shriner by the name of Clint Faulkner happened to be in the waiting room at the time reading a *Reader's Digest* reprint of Bob Greene's column on Tucker.

Faulkner, a real estate broker, had no idea the severely stooped, pigeon-toed boy who made his way toward the restroom was the boy he was reading about. But then Faulkner heard Judi Church refer to the boy as Tucker, and the Shriner put two and two together. He immediately told the boy and his mother that he could get Tucker free medical care that could straighten out his legs.

"I'm sure we can make him walk better, stand taller," Faulkner said.

At first, neither mother nor son believed him. First of all, Judi had been told by doctors years ago that there was nothing more that could be done for Tucker. Secondly, as Tucker told his mother, "ain't nothing free in this world."

They were wrong.

Judi Church had a difficult time believing what Clint

Faulkner told her. So did Terry. Since when is anything in America free? It seems there's always a hitch. The "Free Trip to ——" comes after you buy a car. Even the "Free Coke" takes a fill-up at the pump. But Judi, like the parents of more than five hundred thousand other children, learned that when the Shriners say "free" they mean it.

All care and services provided at the network of twenty-two Shriners hospitals in North America are totally without charge to the patient and family, and no payments are sought or received from any insurance company or government agency.

If specialized corrective procedures would put a strain on a family's budget, children aged eighteen and under of that family are eligible for the Shriners program. That, of course, means every poor and virtually every middle-class family—people just like the Churches.

Where does the money come from to provide the free medical care at the Shriners' nineteen orthopedic hospitals and three burn institutes? Primarily from the three-billion-dollar endowment fund, which is maintained through donations and bequests from both Shriners and non-Shriners. Additional income is derived from each Shriners' annual five-million-dollar hospital assessment and fund-raising events sponsored by Shrine Temples, Clubs, and Units. In 1993 alone, the total budget for the hospitals is $336 million, with the operating budget at $290 million. The construction budget is forty-six million dollars.

Since the inception of the hospitals, more than $2.25 billion has been spent operating the twenty-two hospitals, and more than $511 million on their construction.

And free still means free.

Not long after the Churches talked with Faulkner, Tucker underwent tests at the Shriners hospital in Houston, particularly in the gait laboratory, where videotapes were made of him walking.

It was the first step in the overall treatment that would have cost at least one hundred thousand dollars if there had been a charge.

Nancy Scarborough, the director of the gait laboratory,

explained that it's crucial for doctors treating children with neuromuscular diseases like cerebral palsy to know when the children's muscles contract. Abnormal muscle actions cause deformity and disability. And if the child is sitting or lying down, it's difficult to determine which muscles cause the problem.

So surface sensing electrodes—doctors call the process electromyography (EMG)—were taped to Tucker's skin, and as he walked, the electrodes recorded the timing of muscles. "I felt a little like the bionic man," Tucker says.

It had been taking Tucker an enormous amount of energy to walk. A child without his problem would have been running on a similar amount of energy. To get an idea of how difficult it was for him to get around, Kathleen Price, the director of physical therapy at the Shriners hospital in Houston, suggests you try walking any distance with your knees severely bent.

"It takes so much strength to hold your body upright when it's being pulled down," she says.

With computerized equipment, Scarborough measured the oxygen consumed by Tucker while walking. His change in heart rate was also measured. Those measurements give a kind of "miles per gallon" equivalent for walking. If Tucker had been a car, he'd have had to pay a fine to the Environmental Protection Agency! He was burning up fuel at the rate of an Indy 500 racer. No wonder he could eat like a horse and still be rail-thin.

The Houston gait lab is equipped to look at joint motions in three dimensions. During walking, the joint angles can be precisely measured and recorded. An array of four to six cameras looked at markers placed on Tucker. "I thought about becoming an actor after performing for all those cameras," he says.

The data Scarborough gathered—which identified the muscles that produced his gait abnormalities—helped Dr. Nancy Hadley decide what procedure she'd try on Tucker. The hamstrings, among other muscles, had to be lengthened. That meant they had to be cut, stretched, and put back together. It took two hours of cutting and sewing before Hadley was done. To say that the therapy after the operation hurts would be like saying it hurts to have several root canals without anesthetic. Many a pro athlete—the Houston Oilers gargantuan tackle Doug Smith immediately comes to mind—often can't play for weeks if they suffer just a hamstring pull.

"They do cry when we make them stretch," says therapist Kathleen Price. "You have to remember in Tucker's case, he had never stood up straight before. It was bound to hurt."

Tucker winces as he describes what was done to him.

"They cut me at the front of the knee on both legs and behind the knees and up by the groin. And they took the tendons and ligaments and stretched them out and set them back together. When I woke up from the operation, I didn't feel too bad. But the physical therapy really hurt, since my legs hadn't been straight in sixteen years."

Four days a week, at least two hours a day, Tucker would work with a therapist. "They'd take my legs straight out and then up. And I did side lifts and scissors. Every time they did it, I felt like I was pulling muscles. I would beg them to stop. It hurt so much I couldn't help but cry."

Clint Faulkner came to visit. So did other Shriners. They joked with him, wanted to know when he was going to run in the marathon.

Tucker was in the hospital two weeks. After that, his mother drove him back and forth to therapy every day. At night, his legs were always placed in knee immobilizers so he couldn't bend his legs. "It's hard to sleep that way," Tucker says, shaking his head.

Three weeks after the operation, Tucker measured himself. He was four inches taller, five foot two instead of four foot nine. That's a lot of stretching.

"That might be the fastest growth spurt in the history of man," he says. "They ought to put me in *Ripley's Believe It or Not.*"

David McMahan, director of the orthotics department, made Tucker some special lightweight braces that restricted crouching of the knees. They can't even be seen if Tucker wears long pants. Sometimes Tucker wears them, sometimes he doesn't. "He's all boy," McMahan says. "He's definitely got a mind of his own."

It took a full twelve hours to make the one pair of braces. If his family had had to purchase them, they'd cost a minimum of two thousand dollars.

For the first time in his life, Tucker really looked forward to going to a clothing store. "Having to go buy clothes because he had gotten bigger was a real psychological lift for him," Judi Church says. "He had stayed the same for so long I think he figured he'd never grow."

After Tucker finished three months of therapy on his legs, Dr. Hadley told the Churches that operations on his feet could make him even more mobile. Essentially what the surgeons had to do was to break many, many bones. They would then rearrange the bones in a shape more conducive to walking and pin them together.

"I never knew what pain was until then," Tucker says.

In fact, the pain was so bad that doctors would only perform the operation on one foot at a time. When Tucker woke up from the operation, there was a cast on his foot. He kept begging for pain medication, since the throbbing never seemed to go away.

When it was time to do the second foot, Tucker didn't want anything to do with it. He screamed. He hollered. As he was being carted down the hospital aisle, he tried to grab onto anything along the way to keep him out of the operating room. Judi sobbed.

"If I die, you'll be sorry," Tucker yelled.

Dr. Hadley even asked Judi if she was sure she wanted the operation. Judi nodded yes. She went into the waiting room and cried hysterically. She only settled down when a maintenance man came and sat beside her. "You're trying to give your son a better life," the man said. "I know it's hard to take his pain right now, but you should be proud of what you're doing."

Tucker was in a wheelchair for three months. When they moved to Alvin in 1991, he was still in a chair with casts on his feet. Finally, Judi made him give up the chair. "I got the feeling he was starting to use it as a crutch," she says. "I know it was painful for him to walk, but he was never going to get over it unless he got out of that chair."

Two weeks later Tucker broke his foot. He had been a little too exuberant on the trampoline.

"So that's how he did that," Dr. Hadley says, smiling as she sat in her office at the Shriners hospital. "They never would really say."

Tucker grinned when he told of how he broke his foot.

"My mother told me never to tell how I did that because she was the one who said it was okay for me to use the trampoline."

Hadley, a thirty-eight-year-old physician who was educated at Harvard, Georgetown, and Maryland, wouldn't have said it was okay, but then again she would have been very careful not to hold him back either.

"What has helped Tucker so much in his life is that his family has let him do what he could do," the doctor said. "That really helped build his self-esteem. He was so much better off than many of our patients when it came to his self-image. Letting him be a boy had a lot to do with that."

Whenever Dr. Hadley enters an operating room, she said she treats every kid like her own.

The Shriners Hospitals for Crippled Children attracted her because she wanted to give children with some kind of disability as good a self-image as possible. "Our perceptions of ourselves are so critical to our success," Hadley says.

When Dr. Hadley heard that Tucker felt better about himself than ever before, the doctor's smile almost broke her face. "That's what it's all about," she said, clapping her hands.

Tucker often speaks fondly of the nurses at the hospital.

That doesn't surprise Rufus Peckham, head of the Arabia Temple Shrine in Houston. "We hear so much from people that our nurses are always enthusiastic," he said.

Pam Costens, an in-patient care nurse, came to the forty-bed Houston Unit in the mid-eighties after working in a large diagnostic clinic. She is one of the enthusiastic caregivers that Peckham talked about. She was featured in the Shriners' international magazine, *Between Us*, in January 1992. "I get up in the morning and eagerly look forward to seeing the kids," said Costens. "They are happy and fun to be with. It's a 'charged' atmosphere—exciting, but with a real sense of caring. Because we are small, you get to know each patient—their fears and feelings. And because we are a free hospital, with less paperwork, we have more time to devote to nursing."

Susan Vardaman, an operating room nurse who began her professional career as a teacher, explained what makes the atmosphere at a Shriners hospital so different. "This hospital," she said, "has a 'healthy kid' environment. Patients come here because they have a special problem; they aren't sick or injured. Our hospital is a happy place... For the most part, the kids are enthusiastic, and the families are usually very excited about the chances for improvement in their lives."

Linda Dumoit, who practiced nursing at large hospitals for fifteen years before joining the outpatient clinic at the Houston Unit, sees hundreds of patients every month. "Being in the outpatient clinic, my responsibilities are similar to working with a physician in private practice," she said. "The uniqueness of it is that I see the kids from the time they are very young to age eighteen. Over the years, you really see their progress."

Costens said that because many of the patients require multiple surgeries, "the kids feel more comfortable in this small, close-knit group. They know they will see the same nurses every time they come back. We really care for the kids and the parents seem to sense that... I've heard people express sympathy for the kids here, but we never have a sense of that. This is one place where handicapped children feel completely comfortable. They're accepted... They're just children."

Costens recalls a little boy named Carlos who couldn't walk when he came to the Houston Unit several years ago. He had arthrogryposis and still had to be carried at age five. "Carlos was back here and was running down the hall. Yes, actually running," Costens said. "At a larger hospital, Carlos might have been treated on the surgical floor and then transferred to a rehab floor. I probably wouldn't get to watch the whole progression. Because we are a small, specialized hospital, we see the whole picture. It's so neat."

The nurses at the Houston Unit are ecstatic that Tucker is now often seen driving around Alvin in a jeep. Before the operation he couldn't pass the driving test. His legs wouldn't do what he wanted them to. He's also fond of a certain female.

"He's been hogging the phone with her, but he hasn't brought her home yet," his mother says.

"Oh, come on," Tucker says. "She's just a friend."

Judi sees that her son is much more confident since the operations. "He walks into a place and you can tell he doesn't think everybody's looking at him."

Tucker has stretched to five feet, seven—a five–inch growth over last year. He weighs only one hundred pounds, but that's a lot better than the fifty-six pounds of three years ago. In addition he's doing better in high school in Alvin. Teachers realized right away that his writing problem needed special attention, and Tucker is more comfortable with his studies because of classes he had in the hospital.

The classroom you see inside a Shriners hospital is hardly typical. Students roll into a room in a wheelchair. Others come by stretcher. Still others limp in and take a seat. There are no desks, no school uniforms. Between September and June, patients bring their studies with them so they can keep pace with their classmates in the regular schools. The Houston Independent School

District provides certified teachers. It's a class act.

"Tucker blossomed in a very short time in math because he had one-on-one instruction," Judi Church said. "All that happened because of the Shriners seems like a dream."

The Shriners certainly made a dream come true for Terry Church.

He had envisioned going hunting with his son long before Tucker was born. They'd get out of their sleeping bags right at the crack of dawn, cook some breakfast, and then be off. He'd tell his boy how to pick up a trail, what snakes to stay away from, how to walk quietly in the forest. Just like his dad did with him. They'd smell of mosquito repellent and enjoy the scent of wildflowers. When he was out in the forest, he'd teach his son that Robert Frost poem about two roads diverging in a wood. He'd bet his son would go ahead and take the one less traveled.

Then Tucker was born. His son, the one he wanted so badly, the one he was going to walk with deep into the forest, was lucky just to be alive. No way could he ever go hunting. He'd fall and the rifle would go off and he'd either get killed or kill somebody else.

Terry wasn't upset that they couldn't go for those long hikes—he was so happy that he still had a son—but sometimes when he looked at the boy he loved, a strange sense of sadness came over him. Like the time they went on a camp out with Cub Scouts and Tucker had to stay with the adults around the campfire instead of heading off with the kids. Yet he seemed a happy child. Terry only wished Tucker could get the chance to head off into the trees to see what he could find, experience the joy that comes when a deer suddenly runs by.

On his bad days, Terry Church looked at his son and instead of wondering if Tucker would miss out on the joy of the outdoors, he wondered if he would even make his way in the world. He didn't know if Tucker had the strength to put up with the fools who got their kicks out of picking on someone different.

But then came the reaction of the American public to Tucker's battle with Little League. Throwing out the first ball at the Astrodome, the visit to Palermo—so many things had made Tucker's confidence grow. And then came the operations at the Shriners hospital. Tucker became more sure-footed. Falls became rare. He didn't need a new pair of shoes every month. He grew. And grew. And grew. He started talking to girls. Tucker asked him when they were going hunting. It was incredible, unbelievable, miraculous, magnificent, delightful, awesome! His son was blossoming before his eyes.

To the outsider, the change may not have seemed so colossal. Sure, Tucker had grown a lot. That was obvious. But the attitude change was so subtle, so fine. Yes, Tucker had always been a joker, seemingly confident. But Terry had long sensed the insecurity that comes from being on the outside looking in—the insecurity Tucker tried so hard to hide with his smoking and rock star, who-gives-a-damn-style shrugs. But now, well, his boy had evolved in a wonderful way. He liked school again. He was beginning to have a social life. They could go hunting!

And they did, after Tucker took the necessary weapons training. As they walked the fields looking for dove, they talked about the birds and the bees, football, baseball, cars, flowers, the sun, Robert Frost. There were moments when Terry thought he was in the middle of his old dream. It couldn't be real. But there they were, walking down a trail, looking for birds.

Terry almost forgot that Tucker had had such a hard time walking before. He didn't fall. He didn't even almost fall. When a dove broke out of the tree line, Tucker bagged it. Terry closed his eyes. Miracles do happen, he decided. Tucker got four more birds and his father got so misty-eyed that he couldn't see to shoot. That was okay, there would be other days. There is only one first time to go hunting with your son, and Terry had just done it.

But what if Shriners hospitals cease to exist? Kathleen Price, the ever-energetic director of physical therapy at the Shriners Hospital for Crippled Children in Houston, doesn't even like to entertain the thought. Yet it pops up in her mind more frequently lately. No doubt it's because whenever she speaks to a Shriner, he's always an older gentleman. That's fine, of course, but she wonders how the transition of Shriners from one generation to the next will take place. When she learns that the average age of a Shriner is sixty-four, she's more concerned than ever. Maybe the happiness and contentment she finds in her work provoke the worry. She's been at the hospital for fifteen years, enjoying each year more than the last. Before that she worked there as a volunteer. Even when they have an operation and their muscles scream out in pain, the kids who come to Shriners are enthusiastic and so are their families about the chances for improvement. Yes, they may cry, but they see a better future. That's what makes the work such a joy. This is where she wants to practice her healing craft for the rest of her life. This is where she helped Tucker Church and countless others make their bodies work as well as they possibly could.

Price wonders if she will be able to continue to help kids who need it so desperately. She remembers the little boy who had meningitis and couldn't even hold his head up and who now looks like a normal little kid. And then there was the girl who was a double amputee who had a near-death experience. Now she's in college.

The work done in the Houston Shriners Hospital captivated Kathleen Price when she was in high school. A friend's father was chief of staff and her friend asked her to visit the hospital with her. Right away she saw the outpouring of caring and love, saw doctors and therapists and nurses working closely together because the hospital wasn't of gargantuan size. She found that staffers at the Houston hospital need to know Spanish because they service a large Hispanic population.

She immediately signed up for classes and even majored in Spanish in undergraduate school. When she got her job at the hospital, she was immediately struck by how badly the children wanted to be just as cool as everybody else. They wanted attention badly, not to be left alone as so often happens in society. So she dotes on them, always using the jargon of the children. Things are "cool" or "radical" or "neat." She is, according to one youngster, "the hippest therapist in the history of therapists." Often, she will use the hospital's swimming pool as part of her treatment of youngsters. They love it. Tucker was one of her favorites because of his humor, and because his parents expected a lot from him. Price never allowed any coddling.

She just can't imagine having to leave the Shriners hospital. "It would be so tragic to stop this kind of work," she said. "Think of all the good we do for people, and they're not charged. Think of how wonderful it is to work at a hospital where money isn't an issue. Can you imagine that today?"

It is, in fact, difficult to imagine Shriners hospitals in an era of out-of-control medical costs. Yet they're very real and very wonderful, one of the finest charitable organizations for children ever conceived. As hard as it is to believe, 96 percent of the hospitals' $290 million operating budget in 1993 is used directly for patient care and research at the hospitals, making its philanthropic program one of the best-run on earth. The fact that the Shriners system is so well run obviously makes the possibility of closures all the more sad.

Even though a three-billion-dollar endowment exists for the hospitals—which take one million dollars a day to run—there are frightening signs for the program. Membership in the Shriners, who must first become Masons, fell from a high of 960,000 in the late seventies to less than seven hundred thousand today. In Houston alone, their numbers have dropped from more than eleven thousand to less than nine thousand. And the numbers across the board continue to decline.

"We do need more members to keep the good work going," concedes Mike Andrews, the Shriners' national director of public relations. "We're having a definite membership problem."

There is a long-standing tradition that someone must express an interest in becoming a Mason before the membership process can begin. Masons don't solicit memberships, arguing that someone who shows an interest without being asked will have a more genuine commitment. That may well be true. It is also noble. Before the explosion of non-profit groups vying for membership, not to mention money, the argument made perfect sense. But today there are more than one million organizations listed by the IRS as non-profit.

It is also true that Shriners are reluctant to brag on themselves—they believe actions speak louder than words. Again, that's noble, even refreshing in a country too full of self-promoters who really have nothing but hot air to promote. But if only a few know when something truly meaningful and beautiful occurs, the country suffers.

The fraternity of Freemasonry, of which the Shriners are a big part, is the oldest, largest, and most widely known fraternity in the world, dating back hundreds of years to when stonemasons and other craftsmen working on building projects gathered in shelter houses, or lodges. Over the years, formal Masonic lodges emerged, with members bound together not by trade, but by their own desire to be fraternal brothers. It is much more than a social organization, for members devote millions of dollars and countless hours to charity.

There are four million Masons in the United States.

And America's children definitely need them now.

Just ask Tucker.

"I'll never be able to thank the Shriners enough," he says. "What gets me is that they just do it out of the goodness of their hearts. Those operations I got done let me go hunting, and enabled me to drive. There were so many other kids in the hospital having things done for them, too. We all felt the same way. We all wished we could do something really big for them."

Shriners now agree that the election of W. Freeland Kendrick to head the fraternity as its Imperial Potentate in 1919 gave birth to the soul of the organization—the Shriners Hospitals for Crippled Children.

As Orville Findley Rush's book on the Shriners, *Parade to Glory*, points out, charity work had never been unknown to the group. From their inception, Shriners would deliver Christmas baskets to the needy during the holidays. Toys would be given to children who had none, and Shriners would see to it that many hungry families received food. But they had never done anything on such a grand scale as building hospitals for disabled children. Of course, no fraternal organization before or since has done anything comparable. It is unlike anything ever done in the history of mankind.

In 1919 Freeland Kendrick was tax receiver for the city of Philadelphia. Later, he would be mayor. A masterful politician and devout Shriner, he wouldn't walk into the Philadelphia temple he headed as the Illustrious Potentate—he'd ride in on a horse or a camel or an elephant. Other Shriners loved his act. He was a man with a huge ego, a man who wanted to be loved, a man who believed he should leave a lasting memorial to himself within the fraternity. He dreamed big dreams. And yet as big as his dreams were, it's doubtful that even he could have dreamed that youngsters like Tucker Church would be thanking him today for working to make his dream for the Shriners a reality.

It was a visit to the Home for the Incurables in Philadelphia that made Kendrick think in terms of a new direction for the Shriners.

"What I saw there, what I heard there, and what I sensed there made such a profound impression on me that for days and weeks I could not drive the sad scene from before me," Kendrick wrote. "This visit to the incurable institution prompted the birth of the idea to inaugurate a movement among the Shriners of North America for rehabilitating orphaned, friendless and crippled children."

When Kendrick went to Indianapolis in 1919 knowing he would be elected Imperial Potentate, he asked Philip D. Gordon of Karnak Temple in Montreal, Canada, to give him a hand in convincing the membership that helping disabled children should be a goal of the Shriners. With the war over, Kendrick decided to tie his plan to the patriotic fervor of the Shriners. He saw an institution for children as a kind of peace memorial.

His flair for the dramatic didn't help him in Indianapolis, however. He had made Gordon wait until the last minute of the last session to offer a resolution. That isn't smart when it's hot and sticky and all the members in the hall want to go off to some cool place. Still, Gordon arose to make the resolution that read:

"Whereas it is the opinion of this Imperial Council, in this year wherein the peace of the world has been established, it would be fitting that some lasting and tangible memorial be established showing to the world at large that we as a body of loyal and patriotic citizens from the various sections of the great North American continent and from which thousands of our membership have enlisted and scores have paid the supreme sacrifice in the cause of justice, liberty and democracy, for all of which our beloved order has stood so prominently.

"And whereas, W. Freeland Kendrick, the Imperial Potentate-elect, has already intimated to this Imperial Council his wish that such a memorial, if possible, take the form of a home for friendless, orphaned and crippled children, in which charitable work he has already taken such a keen interest in his home state of Pennsylvania, now be it

"Resolved, that this Imperial Council place itself on record as favoring such a proposition, the memorial to be styled 'The Mystic Shriners' Peace Memorial for Friendless, Orphaned and Crippled Children,' and that a committee be appointed by the incoming Imperial Potentate, with a view of purchasing a suitable site for this purpose and making all other arrangements necessary, and be it further

"Resolved, that a special assessment of one dollar be made on each member of the Order, to be collected by the subordinate temples, in December next, from their membership in addition to the annual dues for 1920, and remitted to the Imperial Recorder when making their annual returns for the year 1919."

The sweating and tired membership didn't even vote on the matter. But the resolution did give Kendrick a proposal to talk about as he traveled to Shrine temples across the country during the year he served as Imperial Potentate.

Kendrick would travel 150,000 miles to talk about his idea with the membership at their temples. The exchanges with Shriners made him confident that one day his dream would become reality. So confident was Kendrick in his art of persuasion that at the next convention in Portland, Oregon, he went even further with his proposal than before. He suggested that a tax of five dollars (instead of one dollar) be immediately imposed on each Shriner to establish a Shriners Home for Friendless, Orphan, and Crippled children and that a committee select a site so construction could begin.

During discussions about his proposal at the 1920 convention, Kendrick noted the reluctance of some delegates to back a resolution for a "home" at a cost of five dollars to every Shriner. He went to the floor to change his proposal.

"I have changed the original recommendation somewhat," he said, "as I believe it will come nearer to meeting with your approval in the present form and will bring about the object desired. I recommend that at this session of the Imperial Council a resolution be adopted authorizing the establishment of a hospital for crippled children to be supported by the nobility of the Mystic Shrine of North America on an annual per capita basis and to be known as the Shriners Hospital for Crippled Children."

Kendrick had been worried that his idea would be tabled, so he struck the word "home" from his resolution and substituted "hospital." In effect, he was creating a carbon copy of a Scottish Rite Hospital in Atlanta, something far more palatable to Shriners. Many Shriners did not like the idea of creating another home or asylum for orphaned children in America. But an institution that would help to straighten out twisted bodies like the Atlanta hospital did seem worthwhile. By the way other delegates began to talk, it became apparent that a facility modeled after the Scottish Rite Hospital in Atlanta did indeed make far more sense to delegates. Kendrick had toured it as had many of them. That twenty-two-bed hospital had opened in 1915 after Dr. Michael Hoke and Forrest Adair, the head of the Scottish Rite bodies of Atlanta, determined it was needed. The rules and regulations of that hospital would become the guidelines for Shriners hospitals. No patient would pay. The patient should not be an adult and, in the opinion of physicians, must stand a good chance of being helped. It would not become a home for orphaned children. It was open to those in need, regardless of color, religion, or nationality.

"It is quite possible," wrote Orville Findley Rush, the official chronicler of the Shriners, "that without the development of the Scottish Rite Hospital in Atlanta, the Shriners hospitals would have never been brought into being."

Hoping to make his proposal even more appetizing, Kendrick also cut the proposed tax to two dollars. Still, his idea faced stiff opposition.

William Bromwell Melish, the Shriner who had played a large role in guiding the Shrine out of near bankruptcy in the 1890s, took the convention floor.

"I want to present my views on this matter," he said, "and I do so with some reluctance, but I do so with the responsibility resting on me as representing the temple to which I belong. I think that this project is one that we ought not to go into at this time. I think it has not had enough consideration. I doubt its practicality... I believe it to be a project that is not within the province of the Order of Nobles of the Mystic Shrine as it is contemplated, for this reason: It is proposed that this home, if established, shall start out to take care of every crippled child that there is in the United States, and care for them by the Order of the Nobles of the Mystic Shrine; not the crippled children of Shriners, or children of any sort that are now the wards of the several temples, but to go outside of this Order and to take every child that may be admitted under the rules that may be established, with a knowledge before us now that there would probably not be more than five percent of them that had anything to do with the families of Shriners. I don't think that a burden of this sort ought to be put upon this Order."

The argument made sense to many Shriners. The expenditure of untold millions of dollars on an enterprise that they knew little about was a huge risk.

But then Forrest Adair arose to speak. It was the speech that made Kendrick's dream come true. It was the speech that ultimately gave Tucker Church and thousands of other North American children better lives. It was a speech with the emotional appeal of Martin Luther King's "I have a dream" oration.

"I arise, unlike my friend, Past Imperial Potentate Melish... with enthusiasm," he said. "I was lying in bed yesterday morning, about four o'clock, in the Multnomah Hotel, and some poor fellow who had strayed from the rest of the band—and he was a magnificent performer on a baritone horn—stood down there under the window for twenty-five minutes playing 'I Am Only Blowing Bubbles.'"

Delegates laughed. "Do you get it?" Adair said. "After a while, when I dropped back into peaceful sleep, I dreamed of a little crippled children's hospital, run by the Scottish Rite fraternity in Atlanta, Georgia, which has been visited by a number of members of this Imperial Council, and I thought of the wandering minstrel of the early morning, and I wondered if there were not a deep significance in the tune he was playing for Shriners—'I Am Only Blowing Bubbles.'

"We meet from year to year; we talk about our great Order; we read the report of the hundreds of thousands of dollars that are accumulated and loaned to banks and paid us for our mileage and per diem, and on our visitations we stop in some oasis and we are taken in an automobile by a local committee, and he first drives us by and shows us, 'This is our temple, our mosque. It is built of marble brought from Maine or Georgia. The lot cost fifty thousand dollars; we could have sold it for two hundred thousand dollars before we built upon it. The building cost us a million, and it could not be put up now for two and a half million.' And we get here and we hear the baritone horn. That fellow told us what we are doing... While we have spent money for songs, and spent money for bands—and they mean so much to us, let us keep it up—you cannot put your finger on a thing that I know of that has been done for humanity that can be credited to the Shrine as an organization."

Rush wrote that "the hush over the auditorium deepened... already there could be no doubt that Adair was delivering an inspired message, a message that was to become known wherever Shriners gathered as the 'bubbles' speech. One member who heard it was so shaken that in later years he purchased three copies of Sir John Millais' famous painting of a boy blowing bubbles, one of which now hangs in the Greenville, South Carolina, unit of the Shriners hospitals."

Adair told his audience that there were four hundred thousand disabled children in the United States who needed help. "Unfortunately," he said, "they are in the almshouses; they are in the homes; they are mendicants; they are paupers; and the best alms you can give is that which will render alms unnecessary.

"...But...we blow more bubbles and sing again 'Hail, Hail, the Gang's All Here... I want to see this thing started. For God's sake, let us lay aside the soap and water and stop blowing bubbles and get down to brass tacks... Let's get rid of the technical objections. Let's blow all the dust aside. And if there is a Shriner in North America, after he sees your first crippled child treated, in its condition, and objects to having paid the two dollars, I will give a check back to him for it myself. I hope that within two, or three, or four or five years from now we will be impelled from the wonderful work that has been done, to establish more of these hospitals, in each reach of all parts of North America..."

Rush wrote that there was thunderous applause for Adair. Just before the issue came up for a vote, Kendrick appealed to the gathering once more.

"The time has come," he said, "when we should do something big. And what can you do as big as to furnish a hospital for a poor little crippled kid? Suppose it is black; suppose it is Catholic; God put it here on earth; it is up to us to help it..."

Again there was much applause. Then Melish, who had been so ardently against the idea, arose once more. "I want to say just one word," he said. "I think I know how this is going. I think the duty of us all, the duty of myself first, is that if this action is to be taken today...that we want to go before the world showing that the vote was unanimous, and this is the way I'm going to vote."

Melish kept his word. There wasn't one "no" vote.

The Shriners were going into a business—the hospital business—that they knew almost nothing about. And when they named Sam Cochran of Dallas as chairman of the committee to handle the project, more than a few people thought they had lost their marbles. Cochran was a solid Mason and Shriner, but he was also a devout Christian Scientist, a religious faith with a system of healing that isn't in keeping with the American Medical Association. No one need have worried. Cochran became a key player in getting the hospitals built.

Along with Cochran, committee members Philip D. Gordon, W. Freeland Kendrick, Bishop Frederick W. Keator, Oscar M. Lanstrum, John D. McGilvray, and John Morison talked with orthopedic surgeons at the nation's great universities. They also talked with the Mayo brothers at their clinic in Rochester, Minnesota. It was Dr. William

Mayo, himself a Shriner, who convinced the committee to build hospitals across North America. He sent an enthusiastic telegram to committee members after their visit: "I approve of the principle of the building of Shrine hospitals for the care of crippled children. Several should be built... The plan is laudable and worthy of the great body of Shriners."

By the end of 1922, ten sites had already been selected for hospitals. While St. Louis was the first choice, legal difficulties in acquiring property meant the Shreveport, Louisiana, unit would be the first to get underway. On September 16, 1922, it opened its doors to a little girl with a club foot who had learned to walk on the top of one foot rather than the sole.

There are now orthopedic units in Chicago, Illinois; Erie, Pennsylvania; Greenville, South Carolina; Honolulu, Hawaii; Houston, Texas; Lexington, Kentucky; Los Angeles, California; Mexico City, Mexico; Minneapolis, Minnesota; Montreal, Canada; Philadelphia, Pennsylvania; Portland, Oregon; Salt Lake City, Utah; San Francisco, California; Shreveport, Louisiana; Spokane, Washington; Springfield, Massachusetts; St. Louis, Missouri; and Tampa, Florida. Shriners Burns Institutes are in Boston, Massachusetts; Cincinnati, Ohio; and Galveston, Texas.

Approximately 467,000 youngsters have been helped in the hospitals since 1922. There have also been 5,638,179 X-rays taken, 4,146,536 outpatient visits, 485,135 operations performed, 595,444 braces and protheses applied and 9,324,431 physical therapy treatments given.

And free still means free.

Many surgical techniques developed in Shriners hospitals have become the standard operating procedure of physicians around the world. Thousands of children have been outfitted with braces and artificial limbs that allow them to get on with their lives. Make no mistake about it: Thousands of children and parents and families would have lived lives without hope if it weren't for the Shriners.

Just ask **Michelle Holdorf** of Davenport, Iowa. She has no legs and only one arm, but because of artificial limbs developed for her by the Shriners, she has been able to live life on the go. She's camped with the Girl Scouts and played trumpet in her high school band.

Ask actor **Pat Morita**, who's best known for his portrayal of Mr. Miyagi in three "Karate Kid" movies, as well as for his work in the television shows, "Happy Days" and "O'Hara." When a child, he was hospitalized at the San Francisco Shriners Hospital for spinal tuberculosis. "The Shrine enabled a kid with no future at the time or any hope of ever walking again to eventually march all the way to an Oscar nomination," Morita said.

Ask former major league pitcher **Rick Rhoden**, who played with the Houston Astros, Los Angeles Dodgers, Pittsburgh Pirates, and New York Yankees. At the age of eight, he cut his right knee on a rusty pair of scissors. His leg became infected. But even after the abscess cleared, he continued to run a fever. The fever led doctors to diagnose osteomyelitis, an inflammatory bone disease. After being admitted to Greenville Shriners Hospital, he was fitted with a special brace. He underwent surgery at age twelve to slow the growth of his good leg, a technique designed to allow his weaker leg to catch up. Until he was sixteen, he made visits to Shriners hospitals' mini-clinics in Miami, Jacksonville, and Tampa. "If it weren't for the Shriners, I don't know what route I would have taken," Rhoden said. "They really made playing baseball possible."

Ask **Tony Volpentest** of Mountlake Terrace, Washington, a quadruple amputee and an outpatient at the Shriners hospital in Portland, Oregon. In September 1992, running on artificial track feet, he won gold medals in both the one hundred-and two hundred-meter sprints during the IX Paralympic Games, an international competition for the disabled, which drew more than forty-two hundred athletes from ninety-two countries. In the hundred-meter sprint, his world record time of 11.63 seconds bettered the old mark by a tenth of a second. In the two hundred, he sprinted a remarkable 23.07, shattering his own record of 23.97-second set earlier in the day. He emphasized that his world record times were made possible in large part by the staff at the Portland unit.

Ask **Kelli Payne** of Cleveland, Tennessee, who never expected to see her daughter **Heather** walk. Afflicted with cerebral palsy, Heather started walking at four years of age—following surgery at the Lexington, Kentucky, Shriners unit. Kelli told the *Cleveland Daily Banner:* "A parent who has a handicapped child has a lot of things to worry about, and it was real hard in the beginning. But, I can honestly say now, between the way I felt then and now, the only difference is I know there are people called the Shriners. And it takes a lot of burden off."

Ask **Suzanne Payne** of Niangua, Missouri, who's so grateful for the treatment the Shriners have given her eight-year-old daughter, **Nichole**, who lost both feet in a 1992 auto accident. The Shriners hospital in St. Louis will pick up the tab for Nichole's prosthetic care until her eighteenth birthday. "Just before Christmas, all Nichole talked about was whether Santa was going to bring her a pair of new artificial feet," her mother said. "Nichole would never have been able to be fitted with artificial feet if it had not been for the Shriners. We certainly owe a lot to them."

Ask ex-heavyweight boxing champion **George Foreman** and his manager/brother, Roy Foreman, who can't thank the Shriners enough for the treatment given to their younger brother **Kenneth**. He was stricken with polio at the age of three and only because of operations at the Shriners hospital in Houston did he get help. "The more we think about what the Shriners did for Kenneth, the more incredible it seems," Roy said. "To help him for free is really something."

George was twelve and Roy six, when polio struck Kenneth. He tried to get up as he always did, but he kept falling. At first his older brothers thought he was kidding. But then they saw that he was drenched in sweat. It

would be a long time before Kenneth walked again—
seven years to be exact. And when he did, it was with
braces.

People who follow George and Roy Foreman's almost
frantic schedule—if George isn't boxing, he's running to
carry out business deals Roy has negotiated—have long
assumed that a background of poverty in Houston has
spawned their Herculean drive.

And it has, to a point.

It's a story that's become part of Americana.

There were seven children in the family headed by
Nancy Foreman, who worked as a short-order cook. They
could never afford to rent more than a two-room
bungalow. Four children would sleep in one bed, three in
another. And the family moved several times a year
because landlords bumped the rent above ten dollars a
week.

If they were just moving down the street, George would
often carry the couch and beds on his back.

Now, it isn't unusual for either George or Roy to be
doing business in Houston in the morning, New York in
the afternoon, and L.A. in the evening. The next day,
they may be in Vegas before dawn, before hitting
Philadelphia and Boston and New York in the evening.
Sometimes they're together, sometimes they're not.
They've met each other in airports across the country
before taking different flights.

Meineke Mufflers now wants George for their
spokesman. Chevy trucks wants George to pitch their
products. McDonald's, Frito-Lay, Nike, Texaco, the state
of Texas, the American Red Cross, the Houston Police
Department—all of them want George.

And then there are the on-going meetings with Chinese
businessmen who want George to fight a title fight there.
On and on the business merry-go-round goes.

And partly it's because of Kenneth. Because George
and Roy, brothers who are as close as brothers can be, know
that their lives can change just as fast as Kenneth's did.

They didn't even have a wheelchair for him at first.

The family carried him everywhere. If it hadn't been for the Shriners hospital in Houston, Kenneth, who now has only a limp, would never have walked again.

When the Foremans' nephew, Charlie Perry Steptoe, drowned in 1992, George and Roy's sense of the fragility of life only intensified, so they don't waste a minute in taking advantage of the opportunities that are now coming George's way. Their families, a church, a foundation, and charities have to be taken care of. After all, tomorrow they may not be able to run after the opportunities.

"What happened to Kenneth was one of the most painful experiences in our family's life," Roy said as he ate soul food at the El Dorado Diner in Houston. "I still can't believe that one day he could run and the next day he couldn't. You have to do what you have to do as fast as you can in this life, because you never know what tomorrow will bring."

Despite the horrors of polio, the Shriners made Kenneth's life story much brighter.

It is fascinating to learn how the Shriners have evolved in their philanthropic efforts. Houston Shriner Jim Hodges, a stockbroker by profession, loves to tell the story of the organization when he delivers talks to civic groups— presentations he hopes will eventually lead to contributions to Shriners hospitals.

According to Hodges, three things occurred during the decade of the 1950s, which had a dramatic effect on the Shrine fraternity: A polio vaccine was developed; the Shrine experienced a tremendous growth in membership; and the endowment fund grew. Wanting to do even more good work at a time when a crippling disease had been virtually wiped out, the Shrine, which had grown from three hundred thousand members in 1920 to nearly one million, sent a committee to the nation's capital in 1959 to find out what the country's number one health problem was. A colonel in the Surgeon General's Office was blunt:

"It is burns. And we know so little about burns, it's embarrassing."

In 1960 the American Medical Association voted to increase research on burns. The Shrine did its own research and learned that two million people are burned each year in the United States, with seven hundred thousand of those being children. Shriners also learned that little was being done to improve treatment.

The Shriners saw a need and decided to fill it. In 1964 they voted to get into the business of treating burned children.

"It was a gutsy decision," Hodges said, "because of the high mortality rate. Our own doctors said we could anticipate a loss of twenty-five percent of our children and, being very realistic, we might lose fifty percent. It was a sobering analysis, but I'm happy to tell you that none of those figures ever materialized."

In 1966 the Shriners opened their first burn hospital in Galveston, Texas, followed by hospitals in Boston and Cincinnati in 1968. All children coming into the Shriners' system with an eighty percent skin surface burn are sent to Galveston. Because time is critical, the admitting process is done over the phone. All Shrine temples have planes available to them to transport the children without delay. In most cases, a parent or grandparent accompanies the child. Transportation, housing, and meals are all provided to the child's custodian free of charge. Again, all medical treatment is free. The cost of operating a burn facility is more than double that of an orthopedic hospital. For example, the cost of operating the Galveston burn center is about $13.5 million while the Houston orthopedic facility costs around $6.5 million.

"It's really worth it," Hodges said, "because we've become the best in the world at burn treatment for children." In fact, the top three burn hospitals for children in the world are: Shrine Burn Hospital in Galveston, Shrine Burn Hospital in Boston, and Shrine Burn Hospital in Cincinnati.

Ten years ago a child who entered a Shrine Burn Hospital with a fifty percent skin surface burn had no better than a fifty-fifty chance of staying alive. Today, the

Shriners are saving children with a ninety to ninety-seven percent skin surface burn. Not long after the Galveston burn center opened in 1966, doctors there worked to save the life of Darla Jansen, who was burned over eighty-five percent of her body when her flannel nightgown caught fire. Her case helped the U.S. Congress pass a law to make all children's night clothes flame retardant.

While the Shriners hospitals have been engaged in research since their first hospital opened in 1922, it was in the early sixties, when the units really stepped up their work in the area. A twenty-one thousand dollar allocation less than thirty years ago has mushroomed into an international research program with a twenty million dollar budget. Studies are underway on how to prevent scar formation and on why drugs for pain work differently on burned children. Analysis of nutrition and lung function in burn victims is also a current project. Research work in the orthopedic field includes the search for the cure for juvenile rheumatoid arthritis; studies on genetics and its relationship to joint and bone diseases; and biochemical and clinical investigations of hereditary disorders of connective tissue.

Shriners hospitals remain on the cutting edge of medical advancements. In the Chicago, Philadelphia, and San Francisco hospitals, there are Spinal Cord Injury Rehabilitation Units (SCI Units) that provide long-term physical, occupational, and recreational therapy. They are the only spinal-cord injury units in the nation designed specifically for children and adolescents that teach independent living skills. A research project underway at the hospitals is called functional neuromuscular stimulation (FNS). FNS has been designed as a tool to restore standing, walking, and hand-grasp functions to paralyzed children.

Using techniques developed by the Russian physician Dr. Gavriel Illiczarov, doctors at Shrine units are now heavily involved in limb-lengthening, something that not only helps a youngster's physical well-being, but his mental well-being. No child wants to limp. The Houston unit has lengthened a young boy's leg four inches.

Not long ago, Shrine doctors in Tampa, Florida accomplished a medical first. A child was born in South Florida with mermaid syndrome, which means that her legs were joined together. The normal life span of an infant born with this condition is three weeks. But the chief surgeon at Tampa Shrine Hospital elected to do a series of five operations in a three-week period. Eventually, Tiffany York walked without any assistance.

In 1984, surgeons at the Shriners Burns Institute in Boston became the first to successfully graft human skin grown in the laboratory over large areas of the human body. The technique saved the lives of brothers Glen and Jamie Selby of Wyoming. They had been burned over ninety-five percent of their bodies after they got paint on themselves and tried to remove it with solvent—a chemical that caught fire. Cultured from postage-stamp-size patches of the boys' unburned skin, the laboratory-grown human skin was applied to half the body surfaces of the boys. It was Dr. Howard Green of Harvard University who developed the technique of "growing skin" in the laboratory. Small patches of unburned skin are removed from the patient. These patches are processed to remove cells, which are placed into a special solution. After a few weeks, the cultures develop into large sheets which can be used for grafting. "Previously in treating burn patients we had covered up to five percent of the body surface with the cultured epithelium (laboratory-grown human skin)," said Dr. Gregory Gallico, one of the Shriners Burns Institute surgeons who operated on the boys. "We had not anticipated covering so large a percentage of the body at this stage of our experience with (the cultured skin). But since the boys had no other hope of survival, we agreed to try it." There simply hadn't been enough unburned skin on the Selby boys for doctors to use the time-tested method of skin grafting from unburned areas of the patient.

Hodges says that when the public learns of the good works of the Shriners, they often leave bequests in their wills to the hospitals. The gifts play a large role in the institutions staying alive and well and ready to help kids like Tucker Church. For example, the will of seventy-nine-year-old Harry Edwards, a former Houston car dealer, bequeathed nearly five hundred thousand dollars to the Houston hospital. "He knew that the hospital had fine doctors who helped children," said his son, Milton Edwards. "And it was very important to dad that it was non-denominational, a hospital that would help everybody."

Sometimes the living give large gifts, too. An Alabama physician was so impressed with the efforts of the Cincinnati Burn Center that he gave the Shrine a twin-engine Beechcraft plane valued at $250,000. An Oregon farmer—he wanted to be called Farmer Brown—was so impressed after a tour of the Portland hospital that he went home and got his briefcase. He then laid it on the administrator's desk. It contained negotiable shares of stock with a value of five million dollars. After an airline crash in New Orleans burned an eight-year-old girl, she was taken to the Shrine Burn Center in Galveston. The insurance company couldn't believe that the Shriners refused payment. That company made a twenty-five thousand dollar donation to the burn center.

A number of football games, including the best-known, the East-West College All-star Game held in San Francisco, contribute their proceeds to the Shrine hospitals. The motto for the game in San Francisco is often quoted: "Strong legs run that weak legs may walk." Since 1925, no one—not the players, coaches, or officials—has been paid. During the week of the game, the players visit with the young patients at the San Francisco Shrine Hospital. Often, after seeing the youngsters, they leave the rooms and burst into tears. Actor Pat Morita, who was hospitalized there as a child when the players came to visit, will never forget what happened: "I still see very clearly in my heart of memories, the fervor, and the excitement of all my young wardmates... We'd make little dolls of wood, fabric, and pipe cleaners, with hand-sewn numbers on them, and give them as momentos to our visitors. I guess I remember even more the football players who would weep quietly to themselves. I understand now those were not tears of pity for us—the disabled—as much as they were tears of humility and acknowledgment of being able to count their blessings in order to carry on in life."

Tucker Church's story with its happy ending is an important testament to the generosity of the Shriners. Shriners lead by example, and there are too few examples in America today of genuine goodness, the kind of behavior Shriners engage in daily, to allow it to pass by without notice.

Abner McCall, the President Emeritus of Baylor, told about his life as a Mason and Southern Baptist in the February '93 issue of *The Scottish Rite Journal:*

"One December day in 1918 during the great influenza epidemic of World War I," McCall said, "my father received a call for help from the wife of a fellow Freemason stricken with the dreaded plague. My father responded to the call for help and tended his Masonic Lodge brother until he died a few days later. My father returned to his home having contracted the highly contagious disease and himself died thereof in a few days. I was then three years old. When I was seven, and my widowed mother's health had collapsed, Perrin Lodge No. 1082...sponsored me and my sister and two brothers for admission to the Masonic Home and School of Fort Worth, Texas. In 1922 I entered the first grade there and remained eleven years as a ward of the home until I graduated as valedictorian of my class in 1933. A Masonic organization gave me the four-year scholarship which enabled me to go to Baylor University, a Southern Baptist University. I was the first member of my family to earn a university degree. I joined Baylor Lodge No. 1235...over fifty years ago and have since served in a score of Masonic organizations. For several years I have observed and been involved in Freemasonry. I have worked in thousands of meetings with Masons.

"I graduated from Baylor University in 1938, and with the exception of four years of absence during World War II, I have been at Baylor ever since as professor, dean, executive vice president, chancellor, and now president emeritus. After enrolling in Baylor University in 1933, I learned about the distinctive beliefs of Southern Baptists and was baptized into the local church. I have been a member of a Southern Baptist church since 1933. For many years I have been a deacon in the First Baptist Church of Waco, Texas, and have taught the same men's Bible class there since 1949. I was elected twice as president of the Baptist General convention of Texas and in 1979 was elected first vice president of the Southern Baptist Convention... In these thousands of meetings of Freemasons and of Baptists stretching back sixty years, I have seen nothing that made my belief and work in the Fraternity of Freemasons incompatible with my belief and work as a member of a Southern Baptist church. From a long lifetime of personal observation and experience, I can verify that membership and work in the Masonic Lodge and Baptist Church have supplemented and supported each other and in no way supplanted nor subverted each other. They conflict only in the mind of a person who subscribes to a perverted version of Freemasonry, the church, or both.

"...Of this I am sure, anyone critical of either the Baptists or Freemasons can select writings by Baptists or Freemasons which are calculated to give one a distorted view of either. No one who does not observe, participate, and experience the life and works of the Church or the Lodge will be able to understand them. Understanding comes not from just talking the talk, but from walking the walk."

There are criticisms of the Shriners and the Masons from many quarters, but the one glaring weakness of these two groups is that they don't promote their good works often enough. Testimonials from some of the five hundred thousand youngsters like Tucker Church or their families—people who've been helped by the goodness of Shriners and Masons should be written about and broadcast. It's hard to believe that an organization with a goodly share of smart men doesn't have more understanding of the power of public relations.

In the magazine, Dr. Norman Vincent Peale, a Methodist minister and Mason, and author of *The Power of Positive Thinking*, offers an important insight into the organization, and strengthens the argument that the Tucker Churches of this world can ill afford to have the fraternity die off. Dr. Peale called his article, "What Freemasonry Means To Me." It reads in part:

"My feelings on my first entrance into a Masonic Lodge are very clear in memory. I was a young man, and it was a great thrill to kneel before the altar of the Lodge to become a Freemason. This must have been the same feeling my father and grandfather experienced before me. And it must have been identical to the one that many great leaders of America and the world felt as they became Masons. Prominent among this select group are George Washington, Harry Truman, and twelve other presidents, as well as countless statesmen and benefactors of humanity.

"...Of course, Masons say that Freemasonry actually begins in each individual Mason's heart. I take this to mean a response to brotherhood and the highest ideals... Freemasonry is not a religion though, in my experience, Masons have predominantly been religious men and, for the most part, of the Christian faith. Through Freemasonry, however, I have had the opportunity to break bread with good men of other than my own Christian faith. Freemasonry does not promote any one religious creed. All Masons believe in the Deity without reservation. However, Masonry makes no demands as to how a member thinks of the Great Architect of the Universe. Freemasonry is, for all its members, a supplement to good living which has enhanced the lives of millions who have entered its doors. Though it is not a religion, as such, it supplements faith in God the Creator. It is supporting of morality and virtue."

It's important, for the media to seek out stories at the Shriners hospitals. There's a poignant Tucker-Church type of human interest story there every day. In 1992 alone, there were 19,299 admissions to the nineteen orthopedic hospitals and 2,116 admissions to the three burn institutes.

Mike Andrews, the Shriners' PR director, noted that the Shriners have taken out full page ads in *USA Today* in an attempt to gain membership. They also have actor Ernest Borgnine, himself a Shriner, making public service spots. Those are steps in the right direction, but the most concerted effort must be made by local communities.

You can count on one thing: Tucker Church will become a Shriner. He will do unto others as he would have them do unto him. "I want every kid to get the same kind of chance I got," Tucker says. "I just can't understand how people who call themselves religious would be attacking people like the Shriners who try to help kids. It just makes no sense."

Chapter 15

Clint Faulkner's home sits less than a quarter-mile from the Summit, the home of the Houston Rockets, a professional basketball team. Outside the arena, youngsters line up to get autographs from their "heroes," athletes who make well over one million dollars a year for throwing a ball through a basket. When Charles Barkley, the Olympic star and top forward for the Phoenix Suns came to town, the lines grew longer than ever. It doesn't matter that he's deliberately spit on a spectator and without provocation roughed up everyday Joes and other athletes.

Just down the street, in the quiet of the dining room in his small, three-bedroom home, Faulkner is on the phone checking on the condition of another child the Shriners have helped. No one knows that a true American hero is at work.

Faulkner is seventy-eight, frail from a colon problem, but still hardy in spirit. Always the bespectacled real estate broker answers the call of his heart.

"To help a child get over something so he can have a better life is what it's all about," he says. "We can do it in different ways, I know. But if we all made a difference just once, helped some troubled kid some way, think of what our country would be like. Do you think we'd have the trouble we have today if people weren't so selfish?"

There is a tear in his eye as he talks about Tucker Church. He finds it difficult to talk and hands over a letter from a fellow Shriner, Walter Lewis, who had read about Faulkner helping Tucker in a *Reader's Digest* article. "What the [*Reader's Digest*] story [about Tucker], going to so many million people must mean to the efforts of Shrinedom, no one will ever know... I'm sure being able to help this lad means a great deal to you. I'm proud of you..."

The fact that Tucker now has more confidence, the fact that the surgeries allowed him to drive a car—Faulkner says it was goals like this that caused Faulkner to become a Mason, and later a Shriner. He had known a generous man in his youth who was a member, and he followed suit. To this day, he believes what William Preston wrote in 1772 is true:

"To relieve the distressed is a duty incumbent on all men, but particularly on Freemasons, who are linked together by an indissoluble chain of sincere affection. To soothe the unhappy, to sympathize with their misfortunes, to compassionate their miseries, and to restore peace to their troubled minds, is the great aim we have in view. On this basis we form our friendships and establish our connections."

"You don't have to be rich to do what Preston wrote about," Faulkner says as he stares out the window. "But if you do it, you sure feel rich."

We all have a very human need, Faulkner says, to find something to which we can feel a living part of, to be appreciated for our contribution in helping others. We shouldn't beat back the feeling, but go with the flow. It is not a sign of weakness, but of strength. The Shrine has given him an outlet to fulfill his needs.

Faulkner looks at a picture of Tucker Church and shakes his head.

"Too many people see Shriners just as riding on small motorcycles during a parade and wearing funny hats," he says. "I wish they understood what we do. Every kid that goes to a Shriners hospital is sponsored by one of us. And we make sure they have transportation and a place to stay free of charge."

The February 1992, *Reader's Digest*, contained Judi

Church's first-person account of what had happened to Tucker since the first article had appeared in the March, 1990, edition of the magazine:

"In March 1990, Clint Faulkner, a Shriner and real-estate broker from Houston, opened his *Reader's Digest* and read an article about my son, Tucker, who suffers from cerebral palsy. Reprinted in 'Heroes for Today' from a newspaper column by Bob Greene, the story told how Tucker, too stooped and pigeon-toed to play baseball with other fifteen-year-olds, was kicked off a team of younger boys.

"Faulkner contacted me immediately... I was already receiving letters from readers across the nation, offering solace, advice and even free driver-education lessons for Tucker, whose condition made it difficult for him to get a learner's permit. I assumed the hospital could do nothing for my son; his back and leg muscles were contracted too tightly. Many physicians had told us there was no way to correct his deformities. However, doctors at the Houston hospital specialize in a surgery that relaxes muscles and soft tissues. Tucker had three operations, performed free of charge, according to hospital policy.

"Today my seventeen-year-old son can walk through a crowd without attracting stares. He can even take Driver's Ed with his classmates..."

Dick Parrack of Tennessee read Judi's account and was so moved that he sent off a letter to Faulkner. If Shriners need any more convincing that they need to let as many people as possible know about their good works, the letter written to Faulkner from the Greeneville, Tennessee, gentleman should do the trick.

Dear Clint Faulkner:
When I read the article in *Reader's Digest*, I just cried. I was so touched by your compassion that I bowed my head and thanked God that He does send angels to help our children.
As I told you today on the telephone, I am a

teacher. When I taught eighth grade, we used to study a unit in literature about heroism. In eighth grade, students are hard to impress. They think old folks such as we are much too old and out-of-date to accomplish anything. The fact is that they are too smart and sophisticated to consider us anything but hopelessly antique. It is hard to impress an eighth grader.

But as I was working on this unit on heroism, I asked my kids to make a list of their heroes. Then the next day, I required them in a discussion to name the people they had listed and to tell why the names were heroes. And as I went around the room, a little girl raised her hand, and in the sweetest voice you ever heard, she said, "My heroes are the Shriners. Without them, my cousin couldn't walk."

It was an electric moment. I could not speak. I shall never forget it.

So you gentlemen not only cure our sick children; you inspire those who are well to follow your example. I am convinced that we learn of God's love through the love of His children. I have learned much from the Shriners.

Thank you, Mr. Faulkner. Thank you ALL.

When I sit across the porch from God, He will ask me what I recall. I shall tell Him about how you stooped to help a crippled child.

                                                    Dick Parrack

When you see Everett Evans from a distance, it's hard to picture him as the Shrine of North America's highest official, its Imperial Potentate. He wears jeans, a white western shirt, a black Stetson, and black cowboy boots. His belt sports a buckle almost as large as his hometown of Tyler, Texas. He's a burly, muscular, six feet, three, not the type you'd expect to see often in a tuxedo. If the customized motor coach he stepped off wasn't carrying the "Shriners Help Kids" slogan, you'd probably mistake him for a tackle who once blocked for another famous Tyler native, the former Heisman Trophy winner and Houston Oiler Hall of Fame running back Earl Campbell. Or you might assume he's the guy who handles security for native Texan, country and western star, George Strait. You get the picture: Evans is a bear of a man! When he met Tucker in Houston and wrapped his arms around him in a hug, Tucker seemed to disappear.

Up close, you quickly understand how the fifty-eight-year-old Evans rose to the top spot in an organization where a big personality counts for so much—he's a good ol' boy with a smile that seems to stretch from El Paso to Houston. You don't have to really look to see that he has all his molars. The firm handshake lingers as long as his drawled greeting: "Well, Tucker, you been out playing ball with Nolan Ryan? Son, why don't you get his autograph for me? I'd be much appreciative." No one can ever say that Evans, who's taken a year's leave of absence from his truck-leasing business, is lacking in charm. It's a quality that comes in handy when the personal touch makes the difference in whether a contribution will be given to the Shriners hospitals. As Imperial Potentate, Evans serves as Chairman of the Board of Directors of the hospitals. The women he meets in the course of his fund-raising particularly enjoy how he pulls off his Stetson when he greets them with a smiling, "Howdy, Ma'am."

He decided to tour the country in a motor coach telling the story of the Shriners through Clint Faulkner and Tucker Church and countless others because many of the Shriners 191 temples are hard to get to. (If he tried to get to some of the small towns by plane, he'd have to land on the highway.) Driving the bus is Shriner Jim Welsh, who's also from Tyler. Evans' wife, Maxine, is accompanying him on the journey that is expected to tally nearly one hundred thousand miles. The bus is outfitted with sleeping quarters in front and back, two telephones, a fax machine, a microwave, and even a trash compactor.

In communities throughout America, Evans is

campaigning for more membership. He tells Shriners that they have to change with the times. More emphasis, he says, has to be placed on activities for the whole family. "With the husband and wife working all the time, people today don't have much time to spend with their kids," he says. "The man, and his wife, are reluctant to have him go to something by himself. I think if we got more basketball goals and swimming pools at our temples, we'd be a lot better off. That way the whole family could be on hand. We have to think of things that everybody can do. I'm thinking real hard of the Shrine starting a soccer league for kids, too. That would really draw families."

He also says that too many temples are away from where people actually live. "Nobody's living downtown anymore and many of our places are down there," he says. "We have beautiful buildings that nobody's using because they're too far away from where people are living. Nobody wants to drive a good distance for a meeting after a long day at work."

Evans—quick to remind the celebrity-conscious that singer Barbara Mandrell's dad, Irby, is a Shriner, as is actress Sandy Duncan's father, Mancil—never tires of stressing that in 1992 the Shriners were selected as a top award winner in the Associations Advance America Awards. These awards are given recognition by the American Society of Association Executives for significant contributions to society by associations in areas such as education, product and safety standards, professional standards and codes of ethics, research and statistics, international activities, and community service. One of four associations to receive the highest level of recognition are the Shriners, who, noted the judges, have relieved the American taxpayer of a two-billion-dollar burden over the past seventy years through their hospital work.

As he walks through the Shriners hospital in Houston— a facility with an active outpatient list of approximately sixty-five hundred children—Evans looks at a young boy who had to have his leg amputated. He's now being fitted for a prosthesis. Tears well in Evans' eyes. "I'm glad we're able to help a boy like that," he says.

The Houston hospital is a teaching hospital that provides training to orthopedic residents from Baylor College of Medicine, the University of Texas Health Science Center Medical School, and Scott & White Memorial Hospital. The hospital provides an outreach clinic every three months in the lower Rio Grande Valley.

In the outpatient section of the forty-bed hospital, Evans noted how colorful its design is. One of hospital administrator Steve Reiter's pet projects is keeping the institution from looking like an institution. He wants the place to have as festive an atmosphere as possible. It's been a successful venture. Everywhere there are stuffed animals, many bigger than the children. The colors reds, oranges, yellows, blues—seem to promise a bright future ahead. The examining rooms are not coldly labeled with letters or numbers. Instead, there are pictures of animals— a friendly tiger, a cuddly teddy bear. When the children go in for casts, they find in the room a stuffed chicken that's so real-looking many kids wonder why it doesn't lay eggs. There is also a window in the casting room that looks out onto the Hermann Hospital Life Flight Helicopter Pad. Since the kids aren't large enough to see out the window by themselves, when they hear the sound of the rotors, they ask to be taken to the window to see the whirlybird. And they are.

Chapter 16

Judi Church's article in the March 1992 *Reader's Digest* sparked the interest of Peter A. Sullivan, a vice-president of the Million Dollar Round Table. If they would tell their story at the Round Table meeting in Chicago, in June 1992, he was sure people would be moved, and inspired to overcome obstacles they might think insurmountable.

He got in touch with the Churches. "Your story speaks to our very heartstrings," he said. At some point in the presentation, Sullivan said he wanted Tucker to share the stage with Ernie Banks, the retired Chicago Cubs Hall of Famer who would also speak that day.

They were flattered, of course, but the idea of speaking before five thousand people practically scared them to death. They might have turned him down if he hadn't also said a significant donation (it turned out be fifteen thousand dollars) would be made to the Shriners hospital in Tucker's name.

They had to help the Shriners, after all they had done for Tucker. But speak before five thousand high-powered businessmen?

Terry Church, never much for talking anyway, said he couldn't because he'd make the family look bad. If Judi and Tucker did it, Terry said, then the Church family name would remain a proud one. He said it with a straight face. Judi, bless her heart, didn't throw the cake she was baking in his face. She'd heard it all now. What should she say in the speech? There were so many people to thank. Tucker took it in stride. Guys who are planning to be disc jockeys can't shy away from a speaking engagement.

Judi became even more nervous when she found out that Hedrick Smith, a Pulitzer Prize-winning correspondent for the *New York Times*, was also speaking. Man, she thought, these were heavyweights she'd have to follow. And Richard Schweiker, the former U.S. Secretary of Health and Human Services, would be in the audience.

What should she talk about? Her mind flashed through memories.

If she wanted to, she knew she could talk about fear, about screaming for help as she stood in the shower. She could talk about the emptiness you feel in your soul when you have an abortion. She could tell people about how your best plans don't always turn out, about how life isn't fair. She could admit that she never thought Paige would get married and now she's married and the loving mother of two kids.

She could try to describe those awful seizures April had had, that still make Judi shudder today. She could recall how she and Terry fell so in love with their foster child Richard that they thought about stealing away in the night with him, and telling everyone how they didn't take in any more foster children after him. Six years is a long time to love and nurture a child, only to have him taken away. That hurts too much. She could talk about how excited and proud she was when Tucker took his first step at age three, how she jumped higher than she ever had in her life when he did. She could share her thoughts about Edythe, dear Edythe, who really was a second mother, who hadn't had much of a childhood of her own.

What about Little League? What should she say about it? After all, Tucker had loved it most of his life. If she told the audience how she felt about that district administrator Goolsby, they might be shocked. Oh, she'd never get over that. Nobody knew just how important

baseball was to Tucker back then. It had been the glue
that held him together. What if he hadn't been able to
play? What if the whole affair hadn't turned out as it
had? Should she tell everybody how scared she was about
what might have happened? Did she dare tell people
what her nightmares were? Did anybody want to know
she worried that if Tucker had been totally stripped of his
confidence, he'd never amount to anything? Should she
let the people know how angry she was that Little League
didn't learn anything from their experience with Tucker
and was still pulling the same stunts on other kids?

How would she tell people just how grand the people
of Palermo are? Just regular folks who saw something
wasn't right and decided to speak up. Her kind of people.
And they didn't even have disabled kids. Just people who
really care about people. As nice as they are, they are still
a mystery to her. People so wonderful, so decent, so caring.
People who call you up on the phone and say, "Here are
some plane tickets. Would you please let us show you a
good time." Wow! Great people.

And Clint Faulkner, how would she speak about him?
Such a modest guy. Just did what he did because he saw a
kid who needed some help. Just like all the Shriners. She
could talk for hours about the Shriners and the medical
staff in their Houston hospital. Nothing cold about them;
always telling you exactly what's going down, always
holding your hand when it needs to be held. She had
never seen doctors, nurses, and therapists work so closely
together before—the multidisciplinary approach, they
called it. She could honestly say that at first she didn't
know whether she'd like the hospital because there's a
clinic-like atmosphere. You wait with a lot of other people.
But then Dr. Red Duke had told her to get off her high
horse, that Shriners hospitals are as good as they come. It
was so true. Better actually for disabled kids. And they
don't make you pay a dime.

As she thought about the three years since Tucker's
Little League scrape, images kept searing through her mind.
The reporters, so many reporters, asking questions. Some

weren't as well-mannered as she would have liked, but all their hearts were in the right place. What to talk about? There was so much. So much to tell. She really didn't want to talk about how Tucker had gotten off on the wrong track for awhile, how some of those tough guys that he thought would stand up for him ended up making the most fun of him.

Maybe she should let people know how Tucker adored his father, followed him all over the house just as eight-year-old Josh does. And what about Josh, the little boy they had adopted a few years ago so Terry could have another son. He means a lot to Tucker. They're close now. Josh has a learning disability, but is starting to do well in school. And Marriah, she's doing great. She and Tucker like to tease each other. Her treating him just like any other "big brother pest" has helped him a lot. So much to tell. How do you tell people what's so important to you in just five, or ten, or twenty minutes? Everything weaves together in the picture. What really concerned her most is that she didn't know if she could do the presentation without breaking down crying, actually bawling right there in front of five thousand people. There was so much pain involved, so many nice people, so much love, so many dreams.

As it turned out, Judi put together a presentation on note cards for her and Tucker that centered on his earliest days, when he was first diagnosed with cerebral palsy. She would tell of the early struggles of getting him to walk. And, of course, they would talk about baseball, about that little ground ball where there were so many errors that Tucker made it all the way to home plate. There'd also be a section on Tucker being recognized even though he was in the Sylvester the Cat costume. Being thrown off the team and the Shriners experience— those would be mentioned, too. Just little tidbits, not much. Maybe, she thought, she could do it without crying.

When the day arrived, the Churches learned they'd be

speaking behind former baseball player Ernie Banks. They listened to the second of twelve children—a man who had picked cotton and read under kerosene lights—say that you have to work at having a slight edge in life to be a winner.

Banks talked about having wrists so quick that he could wait on the ball longer before swinging. Tucker loved it. He was mesmerized by the notion that Banks had actually gotten to do that when he went to the plate. When Tucker went to the plate, he practically had to swing at the pitch as it left the hurler's hand. It wasn't all that easy for him to get around in a hurry.

Banks said the world is full of people with unused talents, full of people who don't dig down to find out what they're made of. "You have to give all you got so you don't have to wonder about what you've got," Banks said. Tucker let out a "Yeah." All the bases in life have to be touched, the Hall of Famer said. The body, the brain, the heart and the soul. Tucker ate it up. He wanted to go shake Banks' hand, but he had to speak next.

The lights came up on Tucker and Judi in the big auditorium. Tucker walked up on stage wearing black hightop tennis shoes with a brown suit. His feet had been bothering him too much from the operation to wear dress shoes. There was applause. (Tucker's eyes looked like those of a deer caught in the headlights.) He and his Mom weren't professionals and that's what made it so beautiful. She talked about the difficulties during Tucker's birth. She smiled and said that he had caused her so many problems that maybe she and Terry shouldn't have fought so hard to save him. Tucker rolled his eyes. The audience loved the "Oh, Mom," routine. They told the story of Tucker being recognized in a Sylvester the Cat costume and Tucker had his timing down just right when he said: "I couldn't figure out how they knew it was me." The audience howled.

They talked about the work done at the Shriners hospital. Judi related that Dr. Hadley had asked her if it was all right if Tucker's feet were broken in three places and then pinned together. Judi remembered that she said, "No problem."

"Not for you," Tucker chimed in. Again, he had a comedian's timing. The audience was loving it. "I gave my permission for them to do it," Judi said. "Your permission," Tucker said in mock disgust.

Judi told of how Tucker screamed all the way down the hospital hall on the way to the operating room, how he yelled, among other things, "If I die, I'm going to come back and get you."

Tucker was at his best when he talked about why he wants to become a disc jockey. "How hard can it be to push the play button? I do that now in my bedroom."

Judi wept as she delivered her last line.

"I think somewhere in the back of Tucker's mind, one reason he wants to work for a radio station is that no one will ever know Tucker Church walks funny."

Judi and Tucker did something that even the most experienced professional speakers have a hard time doing. They had managed not to get overly maudlin with a poignant subject. Oh, Judi had a tissue to wipe her eyes with, and she shed a few tears.

There wasn't, as they say, a dry eye in the house. Five thousand people stood up to applaud. It was, in Tucker's words, "awesome." So it was. Within seconds, Ernie Banks, dressed in a Cubs uniform, came out to hug Tucker. So did Dan Pascual and Ron Karkabis from the Chicago White Sox. Pictures were taken of Tucker getting the check for the Shriners.

William T. O'Donnell, the president of the Million Dollar Round Table, congratulated the Churches on their presentation, calling it "superb." Other insurance men, John Prast and Mark Jones, offered their thanks for the inspiration.

Late into the night Tucker talked to insurance men about baseball.

And he had a few jokes to tell.

"Did you hear about the Chicago track star who won a gold medal?"

"He was so proud of it he had it bronzed."

"Why did the Chicagoan buy only one snow boot for winter?"

"He heard there was going to be only one foot of snow."

One man he met turned him on to poetry. It was the last thing Tucker expected out of the trip.

Yes, Godfrey L. Smith III made a profound affect on Tucker. And not at all because Smith had been selected MONY's Man of the Year—Tucker knew nothing about the company that has over twenty billion dollars of assets. Smith's clever card trick was okay, but nowhere near as good as his poetry.

An insurance agent who writes memorable poetry? Why not?

Of the sixteen poems Smith gave Tucker as a gift, there are three that he reads regularly. "They make me feel good," Tucker said.

One poem brings tears to Tucker's eyes as he recites it:

THE ONLY WAY TO FLY...

> It's strange... that you view me... as handicapped,
> When my problems... seem far less than yours!
> Oh, it's true... that I have limitations,
> Need help... to perform certain chores.
>
> But then, I'm not the one who's afraid to ask,
> Who pretends... he's no need for another.
> Content... to live a life that's a sham,
> No room... in my world for a brother.
> So before you look at my limbs with pity,
> And assume... there's a lifelessness there,
> I may not be the only one... who's partially
>   paralyzed,
> Though... I'm the only one who's still in the
>   chair.

There are far more in this world... who are
              crippled by fear,
Confined... by goals... far too small.
Who are battered and broken... stoop when
              they walk.
Simply... because they fail... *to stand tall*!

In truth, I have freedom... not confined to this
              chair,
Like a spirit... I can soar... like a dove!
The source... of this remarkable motivation?
They're the wings... of a power... called Love!

"One of the great things that came out of the fight
with Little League is getting to meet so many people,"
Tucker said. "People like Mr. Smith—I guess I would have
never gotten the chance to meet him unless I had moved
to Virginia and needed some insurance."

Tucker is truly happy to have met Smith, one of those
unsung Americans who make the country work. In
Virginia, among other things, Smith has served as
President of the Big Brothers of the Peninsula, the Mercury
Lions Club, and the Peninsula Salvation Army Advisory
Board, as well as working as a volunteer counselor and
teacher at the Hampton City Jail. Smith, who calls Tucker
"a real winner," recently sent the teen a poem that Tucker
put up on his wall:

WIN...

When your body's aching... and your muscles
              strain,
And you think... you can't hold out... to gain
One second more... an ounce of strength...
To stretch the sands of time in length.

Remember! Why you've come this far.
Whose reputation... surrender... would mar...
And then... Hang on... Dig deep... and Strain!

The rich reward... of victory's gain
Is worth the price... so many have paid,
To get you to this place... you've stayed;
By gumption... guts... hard work... and pain,
You can't by coasting... still remain.

So out of love... for others... prior,
Match price... for price... their deep desire,
To see The Gold... rest on your chest,
And know... the effort's worth your best,

Which... you'll discover... IF... you'll trust,
To believe in others... yourself... you must;
Risk revealing... who... you are,
To unveil... tomorrow's Superstar...

Not formed nor cloned... but born of labor,
Hard work... and sweat... sustained by neighbor;
Who hired the coach... and built the school,
Created order... where chaos ruled.

So before you quit... what if they had?
What kind of world... would await your lad?
This isn't merely a match... a game,
Its course... may determine... much more than
        fame.

So if Success... is to... remain,
Perhaps, we too... must endure... sustain;
Those values... which... our legacy has been,
Suck Up the Pain... Hang On... and WIN!!!

Naturally, Tucker loves a Smith poem—entitled A Love of the Game—about baseball. "He seems to have a lot of the same feelings I have about the game," Tucker says. "I really love the game, too."

It is high noon in Alvin, Texas, as Tucker wheels his jeep into the driveway of his parents' home. He's been off visiting the girl he calls a "close friend," sixteen-year-old Christy Byrne, a five feet, six inch, blue-eyed blonde, who's a key member of the Alvin High School drill team. If you didn't know who he was and someone told you he just finished his radio show, you'd have no reason to disbelieve it. As he climbs out of his jeep, he sounds as though he's polishing an introduction: "This is KRBE, the station that's designed to put more cut in your strut, more pride in your stride."

Tucker wants to show his visitor Alvin. He couldn't be more upbeat. "Hey," he says, "did you know there's a farmer outside Houston who's won such a reputation as a liar than even the pigs don't come when he hog-calls?" Even the tires throwing up loose gravel can't drown out his laugh. Driving through the city of 20,000, he talks about his future and about baseball. He has his baseball glove in the back seat. He never knows, he says, when he and his younger brother Josh might go over to the field for a pick-up game. The mere mention of the glove brings a smile to Tucker's face. And memories—so many memories. He loves, he says, even the way the glove smells. He had had the same glove for years. His lucky glove, the one that he had caught a scorching line drive with—the glove he once threw on top of the roof and had to go get. He'd put oil in the glove so it got good and soft, and then it always smelled special like nothing else in the world. He would always remember that smell. Only Christy's perfume smelled better. He remembered the time he'd caught a fly ball he had to run for. He saw it from the crack of the bat as it went to his right. He was in left field and started running as fast as he could. At first, he could hear people yelling. Twice he almost fell down, but he kept going. He just knew he was going to catch it. Then he saw his teammate slide in front of him, yelling,

"You take it!" The ball hit his outstretched glove, bounced against his cheek, and then back into his glove. What a catch! All his teammates came to mob him.

And then there was the time he was playing second and the ground ball bounced up and hit him in the nose, and he still threw out the guy at first. He got a bloody nose, but he still did his job. He felt so good about that. And there was the time he couldn't get his glove onto a short pop fly, but he did get his hand on it, and he caught it! You didn't even see major leaguers do that. Once he hit a ball all the way to right field and the fielder caught it. It may have been his best hit.

Tucker stops his jeep at a Sonic Drive-in, the place he often comes with Christy and his friends, Shawn Spruill, Steve Haynes, and Kenneth Norwood. As we eat our burgers, Tucker grins. "Baseball's still got a hold on me, doesn't it?" he says. "I think I'll go from being a disc jocky to a baseball broadcaster."